Benjamin Stillingfleet

Principles and power of harmony

Benjamin Stillingfleet

Principles and power of harmony

ISBN/EAN: 9783337043018

Printed in Europe, USA, Canada, Australia, Japan

Cover: Foto ©ninafisch / pixelio.de

More available books at **www.hansebooks.com**

PRINCIPLES AND POWER OF HARMONY.

AND IT CAME TO PASS, WHEN THE EVIL SPIRIT FROM GOD WAS UPON SAVL, THAT DAVID TOOK A HARP, AND PLAYED WITH HIS HAND: SO SAVL WAS REFRESHED, AND WAS WELL, AND THE EVIL SPIRIT DEPARTED FROM HIM. I. SAMVEL XVI. XXIII.

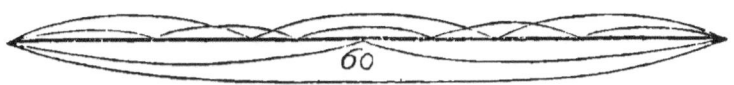

LONDON:
PRINTED BY J. AND H. HUGHS:
AND SOLD BY S. BAKER AND G. LEIGH, YORK-STREET;
B. WHITE, FLEET-STREET; J. ROBSON, NEW BOND-STREET;
AND J. WALTER, CHARING-CROSS.
MDCCLXXI.

PREFACE.

THE high opinion which I had long entertained of the music of Sig. Tartini, together with his great reputation over all Europe for many years, made me expect something extraordinary from a Treatise published by him, intitled, Trattato di Musica secondo la vera Scienza dell' Armonia. I always imagined he had principles unknown to other Artists in his way. A superior effect must imply a superior cause. In this opinion I was not disappointed. I found his treatise full of many new and well-founded doctrines, practical as well as speculative. To give some idea of these, is the design of the following short Piece.

As there are many parts of the original very complicated, and difficult to comprehend, and as the language it is written in is not generally understood, I thought it would not be unacceptable to some lovers of Music, to see his principles explained in a more easy way: But my design is not to render his treatise useless to musicians by profession, which could not have been done without almost an entire translation, and a great number of plates; on the contrary I mean to excite such persons to read and study the original, as the best means to make some improvement in one of the most delightful of all arts.

PREFACE.

I doubt not but the greateſt part of my Readers will be offended with ſome of Tartini's ſtrict notions, particularly thoſe contained in the 5th chapter, as being ſo very oppoſite to every thing they have been taught to admire: but before they condemn, I deſire they will calmly weigh and conſider them — that they will reflect that faſhion is never the teſt of truth, though they may ſometimes happen to coincide—and that theſe ſtrict notions do not come from a dull plodding artiſt, who for want of genius would willingly circumſcribe the flights of thoſe, who are bleſſed with ſuperior talents, by the rules of a barren and narrow theory; but from one who, I may almoſt ſay, led the way in the flowery regions of harmony, and of whom moſt artiſts are but diſtant followers. When an artiſt ſpeaks ſlightingly of that in which he excels, one may ſafely, I imagine, rely upon his opinion.

But the Reader will perhaps be apt to think, that inſtead of making an apology for Tartini, I ought rather to make one for myſelf, as having taken the liberty to diſſent ſo frequently from him; and that too without reſerve. But I hope it will be allowed that one may very ſincerely admire an author, and yet freely cenſure him. Thoſe who think otherwiſe, know very little of that mixed character, which is not uncommonly found in men of ſuperior talents. When Huygens, Coſmo. lib. 2. p. 131. ſays of Kepler. 'But he 'ſtood in need of theſe (fantaſtical) ideas, in order to con'firm his coſmographical myſtery, &c.' And again, 'All this myſtery, if well conſidered, appears to have 'been

PREFACE.

' been a dream arising out of the Pythagorean or Platonic
' philosophy; nor do his proportions answer, &c.' When
we read these passages, can we suspect that Huygens had
not a just regard for the great and excellent Astronomer
whom he so freely censures? The same may be said of Mr.
Maclaurin, whom I have quoted in the following pages,
and who, on the same occasion, uses the same language as
Huygens. It appears by many passages in my author, that
he also had strongly imbibed the notions of Pythagoras and
Plato; nor is it extraordinary that this should happen to a
musician, when we consider that their philosophy was
founded on harmonic principles. This was the very characteristic of it; and so truly great and sublime it is in many respects, that one would be apt to think it originally
flowed from a higher source than mere human notions;
and that it was the obscure remains of the patriarchal religion, which undoubtedly was very early established in
Ægypt, and from thence was brought into Greece by Pythagoras, but delivered in a mystical and symbolical method as to particulars. This mystical method, I am apt
to think, contributed greatly to mislead Tartini. Platonic
numbers and figures had made a strong impression on his
mind, and set him upon the very laborious task of deducing every thing in music from abstract ideas; but these
were accompanied with such important physical experiments, so fine an ear, and such a thorough practical knowledge of his art, that he seldom draws wrong consequences.

I trust

I trust I shall not be thought to have mispent my time in writing on this fine art, if I have, in any degree, contributed towards clearing up the principles of it. To take away all doubt in relation to this point, from those who are unacquainted with the history of music, I will give a list of some writers upon it. Democritus, Archytas, Plato, Antisthenes, Aristotle, Aristoxenus, Theophrastus, Plutarch, Euclid, Ptolemy, Varro, St. Austin, Boethius, Cassiodorus, Albertus magnus, Pope John XXII. Guido, Mersennus, Galileo, Descartes, Huygens, Wallis, Lord Keeper North, Euler, Smith, all of them men of very considerable character in their times. In such a list of writers who would be ashamed to be enrolled, even though it were allowed, that on this occasion they descended below their usual dignity?

Ptolemy very justly says, 'That it is the business of
' contemplation and science to shew that the works of na-
' ture are constituted according to some proportion and
' settled order, and not at random, or as it were, by chance.
' But particularly this ought to be done in relation to the
' finest of her works; such as these senses that approach
' the nearest to reason, viz. the sight and hearing.' Harmon. p. 7. In this I have laboured and endeavoured to reduce to a greater degree of facility, an art which has hitherto been involved in calculations formidable enough to deter every common reader from attempting to understand it, calculations that seem to me more ingenious than useful, and therefore more fitted to obstruct than to advance its improvement,

provement, for want of that simplicity which ought to accompany every art, and every science.

But simplicity cannot be obtained without a just and well-founded system; and to form such a system, is to create, according to the Platonic sense of that word. For it is to take the confused elements of things, and bring them into order. Now to do this is to make them the objects of knowledge. For knowledge, properly speaking, is seeing the properties, connections, and dependancy of one thing on another; it is seeing effects in their causes, and therefore it is foreseeing natural events, and consequently it is knowing the use of things, and in what manner they are to be applied, in order to answer our purposes.

It is with the utmost humility, and a consciousness of the great distance between the great Galileo and myself, that I presume to apply to the doctrines in this treatise, what one of the interlocutors in his dialogues is made to say of some of his discoveries. ' This extreme easiness wherewith
' you manifest the most abstruse conclusions, will be
' apt to lessen the value they had whilst they lay hid
' under contrary appearances: Thus I dare say it is with
' the generality of mankind; they have a much less esteem
' for that knowledge that is so very easily acquired, than
' they have for that, about which more tedious and puzzling debates are bandyed to and fro.'

EXPLICATION

OF

Some TERMS used in the following PIECE.

HEXACHORD, in the following piece, signifies the first 6 notes arising in the harmonic series; vide fig. 1, example 1. This word generally means the first 6 notes in the diatonic scale; viz. C, D, E, F, G, A.

FIRST BASE signifies the key-note, suppose C.—The SECOND BASE signifies the 3d of the key-note, or E.—The THIRD BASE signifies the 5th of the key-note, or G.

TETRACHORD signifies the interval of a 4th, as from C to F.

MONOCHORD signifies a musical string that is stopped by pressing on a moveable prop.

STRING OF THREE SOUNDS signifies a string that is sounded without stops, and which always gives the 12th and 17th (i. e. 5th and 3d when reduced to the same octave) along with the sound of the whole.

TRUMPET MARINE signifies a string sounded by touching it gently without pressing on a prop. In this the longest part of the string is struck, and the shortest part sounds.

The TWELFTH, in music, means the 5th above the octave, which is frequently called the 5th.

The SEVENTEENTH means the 3d above the octave, and is frequently called the 3d.

The DIATONIC Scale, which is also called the system of the 3d major, or sharp 3d, is that which has neither Flat nor Sharp belonging to it, as being the primary exemplar of the octave.

The CHROMATIC Scale, which is also called the system of the 3d minor, or flat 3d, is that which has Flats or Sharps, or both, belonging to it, as being a deviation from the Diatonic, and therefore necessarily subject to Flats and Sharps, i. e. alterations as to gravity and acuteness.——N. B. CHROMATIC, in the vulgar sense of the word, means no fixed scale at all, but a variable succession of notes passing from one key to another, as genius or fancy leads.

When a series of notes is marked by great letters, as G, B, D, the first note is always supposed to be the lowest, and so to ascend regularly; but when small letters are mixed with the great ones, the small letters represent the high notes, and the contrary; thus, suppose the following letters, *c* E *g* C, here you fall from *c* to E, then rise to *g*, and lastly fall to C.

IN the account I propose to give of Tartini's Treatise on Mu- *Intro-* sic, I shall have very little to say on his Introduction; which *duction.* consists of numerical proportions and calculations only; though he says it contains the foundation of all the respective de- *Numerical* monstrations employed by him. But as I shall make use of other *proportions.* principles, in their nature I hope not less certain, and much easier to be comprehended, I think it is not necessary to enter into any detail on this subject. Says he, " I allow and confess that " the method employed by me has some novelty in it, and con- " sequently some difficulty; but I also know that they are ne- " cessary." As to their novelty and difficulty, they must indeed be both allowed by every one; as to their necessity, that point must be left to the decision of proper judges. I am sorry to be forced to own, that he sets out in a manner that will at first sight offend every mathematician, and hinder many from paying that regard to his book, which it deserves. He wanted, on this occasion, a little of that skill in writing, which he shews in so eminent a degree in composing, I may say in playing; for so it is reported of him; viz. the skill of passing from note to note, and from tone to tone, almost insensibly. Instead of this art, which was so necessary in writing to mathematicians; for to them he must write or nobody; he begins with a strong discord, by thrusting into his proportions a geometrical mean, as he calls it, which he owns is no mean at all, as it really is not.

[2]

INTRO-
DUCTION. "Of this geometrical mean," says he, "people have no idea, nor can have, as being contrary to the definition and common meaning of that term." After this confession, and after having granted to mathematicians all they can wish; says he, we must now see what they ought to give up in their turn to musicians. This idea is quite new! mathematicians will be apt to reply, with indignation: Give up and compound for error! why we retire into the regions of demonstration in order to avoid it! But however harsh Tartini's language may sound to delicate ears, there is at the bottom no great harm in calling things by wrong names, provided notice is given; and this is the case here. For the rest, Tartini must have employed great thought and labour throughout his whole treatise, in order to press such calculations as he uses into the service of music, for which they seem very ill suited. This is all I have to say on the Introduction; as entering into a detail would be both tedious and useless. Those who are curious in such matters may have recourse to the original, which will be necessary to my readers on many occasions. I now pass on to Tartini's first chapter, which contains an account of all the phænomena on which music is founded; and amongst them one quite new and very important.

CHAP. I.

§ 2.
String of 3 sounds.

Fig. 1. example 1 or 2.

Tartini begins his first chapter with giving an account of a well-known phænomenon; which is, that a musical string, which being struck, one would imagine should produce but one sound, yet in reality produces three; viz. the sound of the totality, and besides that its 12th and 17th, commonly called the 5th and 3d, which are in the harmonic proportion $1, \frac{1}{3}, \frac{1}{5}$. The Trumpet Marine, the Common and French, or rather German Horn, have no notes but what are expressed by $1, \frac{1}{2}, \frac{1}{3}, \frac{1}{4}$, &c. Vide fig. 1. example 1 or 2. The Trumpet Marine is played upon,

not

[3]

not by pressing down the string on a finger board, as on the violin, violoncello, &c.; but by touching it laterally and gently with the finger, which serves as a rest or prop, in such a manner, that the vibrations of the parts of the string, when struck, may pass on freely to the part not touched, the sound of which will be chiefly and almost solely heard. Now unless the part of the string which is not struck be an aliquot part of the whole, no distinct sound will be heard at all, but a jarring disagreeable noise. I call $\frac{1}{2}, \frac{1}{3}, \frac{1}{4}$, &c. aliquot parts of unity, because they are generally called so, though Tartini rejects the term; however his way of expression comes to the same.

CHAP. I.

§ 3. *Trumpet Marine*, Fig. 2 *further explained.*

For the better understanding my meaning in relation to the Trumpet Marine, see plate fig. 2, where the line A B represents a musical string; let A C be one half, A D one third; A E one fourth, of the whole, &c.; stop at C with the finger, as directed above, and strike C B; and A C, which is not struck, will sound. Again, stop at D, and strike D B, and A D will sound. Lastly, stop at E, and strike E B, and A E will sound; and so in any other part, where the short part of the string is an aliquot part of the whole. But if a part of the string, as suppose A F, is not an aliquot part, no distinct sound will be heard, as Tartini undertakes to prove, and is known to be fact. By an aliquot part of any quantity, as of a line, a surface, &c. is meant such a part as will measure the whole without a remainder. Thus an inch will measure a foot, without a remainder, but not a foot and half an inch. I shall consider this subject more particularly afterwards. I have dwelt longer on this phænomenon than perhaps may be thought necessary, considering it is so well known; because I shall make great use of it in the course of this piece; and therefore desire such readers, to whom it is new, to attend particularly to it; assuring them, that they will be able to understand the principles of music by the help of this phænome-

non,

Chap. I. non, when a little farther explained; and one or two others, full as eafy.

§ 4.
Organ.

Tartini obferves, that the pipes of an organ that found, when the full harmony is ufed, are many and various in pitch, and yet but one found is heard, which is the loweft. Their difpofitions are different, according to the different ftops, but all harmonic; it being impoffible otherwife to produce this effect. The notes muft be C, C, G, C, E, G, or fome of them. I fhall have occafion to mention this, or a fimilar and very important phænomenon, in another place.

§ 5.
Ofcillation of ftrings.

Suppofe there is a number of fonorous ftrings of equal thicknefs, and of lengths, as the fquares of the harmonic feries, $1, \frac{1}{2}, \frac{1}{3}, \frac{1}{4}$, &c. i. e. as $1, \frac{1}{4}, \frac{1}{9}, \frac{1}{16}$, &c. and that thofe ftrings be fufpended, and an equal weight faftened to each; the founds produced by ftriking them will be C, C, G, &c. as mentioned in the laft §, according to the number of ftrings. The ofcillations alfo of thefe ftrings will coincide, but with this condition, that while the ftring 1 ofcillates once, the ftring $\frac{1}{4}$ will ofcillate twice, the ftring $\frac{1}{9}$ three times, the ftring $\frac{1}{16}$ four times, &c. The very fame thing will happen, if we fuppofe a feries of ftrings equal in length and thicknefs, and a weight as 1 be faftened to the firft, a weight as 4 to the fecond, a weight as 9 to the third, a weight as 16 to the fourth. We fhall have the fame founds as before, and the fame coincidences, example 1 or 2, fig. 1.

Fig. 1. ex. 2.

§ 6.
Harmonic unity.

" Thefe," fays Tartini, " are phænomena commonly known;
" their indication and fignification are phyfically manifeft. The
" ftring of the monochord, or of the harpfichord, although one in
" itfelf, produces three founds of the harmonic feries. The Trum-
" pet Marine, the Common Trumpet, and the German Horn, nei-
" ther have nor can have any founds but what arife from unity as
" harmonic.

" harmonic. The pipes of the organ, though different in pitch,
" yet form but one sound, when they are disposed harmonically.
" Sonorous strings suspended, when they are in harmonic pro-
" gression in their sounds, are reduced to unity in their oscilla-
" tions. Therefore the harmonic system reduces diversity to
" identity, multiplicity to unity; and simple unity divides itself
" harmonically, as appears by the three sounds that are heard
" upon striking a string, see § 2. Therefore unity, considered
" in any respect whatever, is inseparable from the harmonic
" system. The consequence is perfectly legitimate, because it
" arises from nature, and therefore is absolutely independent on
" the human will."

The last phænomenon which Tartini mentions is quite new, and proves, he says, the foregoing doctrines wonderfully; and goes still farther. It is as follows: Two sounds being given on any musical instrument, which will admit of their being held out for any time, and of being strengthened at pleasure, as on the trumpet, the German horn, the violin, hautboy, &c. a third sound will be heard. On the violin, let the notes C E, C✻ E, B E, B G, B♭ G, be sounded with a strong bow, the third sounds will be heard as in plate fig. 3. and are marked by closed notes or crotchets. The same thing will happen if the same intervals be sounded by two players on the violin, distant from one another about 29 or 30 feet; always using a strong bow, and holding out the notes. The auditor will hear the third sound much better, if placed in the middle between them, than if nearer to one than the other. Two hautboys will produce the same effect, placed at a much greater distance, and even when the hearer is not in the middle, and still more if he is. From this phænomenon he deduces all the third sounds arising from simple intervals, that together compleat the harmonic series, as far as it

CHAP. I.

§ 7. *Third sounds.*

Fig. 3.

Chapter I. is used in practice. The 5th gives the third sound unison to the lower note; the 4th gives the 5th below the lower note, &c.; but I shall not enumerate all the third sounds, though the detail is extremely curious and instructive, because they would be ill comprehended without plates, and many plates do not come within my design; I must therefore refer the musician to the original, which, if he has any genius, will be of great use to him in many respects besides this. I will just observe, that supposing any interval in any key is sounded, if a 4th or a 6th of the fundamental note comes into the chord, we have always the 4th of the fundamental for third sound; in all other cases we have either the fundamental note itself, or the 3d of it. I will likewise observe, that the smaller the interval, the farther distant is the third sound; insomuch that the third sound to the interval of the semitone minor G*, is the 26th below the lowest note. Ought not this to regulate the bass in common practice? *N. B.* There is one exception to the progression above-mentioned, which is when the chord of the 3d major is reversed.

§ 8.

Musical sketch with third sounds.

He then gives a short sketch of music along with the third sounds for a bass, in which he has introduced a new interval into music, new in reality, though not so in appearance; of this an account will be given in the proper place. In his observations on that sketch there is a passage which puzzled me for some time, and may possibly puzzle others; for which reason I will explain it. He reckons, page 17, D$^\flat$, G*, amongst the diminished 3ds, which, says he, will appear to be such, by putting G* above. He means to say, that putting G* in its place, instead of putting it above, the diminished 3d, will appear; and so it will if you place every note in its natural order; for then they will stand thus, E, G*, B, D$^\flat$; where the two last notes form the 3d above specified. He observes on these

third

third sounds, that if any adjoining two simple intervals in the harmonic series $1, \frac{1}{2}, \frac{1}{3}, \frac{1}{4}$, &c. be sounded, the third sound will always be that of half the string; from whence he draws some consequences which I will pass over at present, and perhaps entirely.

CHAP. I.

We have now gone through the first chapter, which contains the most curious and important discoveries ever made in music; discoveries fully sufficient to account for every thing practised, or practicable, in that art. Some of my readers may perhaps desire to know something about the history of these discoveries; which desire I will endeavour to gratify as well as I am able. My account, I foresee, will be very imperfect; for want of books and previous inquiries; but even an imperfect one may perhaps be better than none, especially as I believe that it is not to be found in any one book.

§ 9. *Accounts of discoveries in music.*

Unless the proportions of intervals in music are ascertained, no music can be noted; unless it is noted, none regular can be had. Noting in music is as important, as an alphabet, or something analogous, in the other arts and sciences. But how this ascertaining and noting were to be brought about was the difficulty. That the Greeks looked upon the first as a difficulty, and a great one, appears by their attributing its discovery to mere chance; and that the second, *viz.* noting, was not more ancient, in their opinion, appears by their attributing it likewise to Pythagoras. Vide Meibom. in Aristox. p. 105.

§ 10. *Noting of music.*

The first discovery then, in order of time as well as importance, was that mentioned § 5; *viz.* that if there be a series of strings, equal in length and thickness, &c. and a weight as 1 be fastened to the first; a weight as 4 to the second; a weight as 9 to

§ 11. *Discovery of intervals.*

the

CHAP. I. the third, &c. we shall have the same sounds produced, upon striking them, as arise upon the monochord when the whole is sounded, or the parts at the points $\frac{1}{2}$, $\frac{1}{3}$, $\frac{1}{4}$, &c. respectively. This discovery, or what is similar, is by the Greeks attributed to Pythagoras, and many circumstances attending it are related. The story is so well known, that I should not trouble the reader with it, if I had not particular reasons for so doing. The story then is as follows:

§ 12.
Hammers of Pythagoras.

Pythagoras one day meditating on the want of some rule to guide the ear, analogous to what had been invented to help the other senses, chanced to pass by a blacksmith's shop, and observing that the hammers, which were four in number, sounded very harmoniously, he had them weighed, and found them to be in the proportion of 6, 8, 9, 12. Upon this he suspended four strings of equal length and thickness, &c. and fastened weights in the above-mentioned proportion, to each of them respectively; and found that they gave the same sounds as the hammers had done; *viz.* the 4th, 5th, and octave to the gravest tone; which last interval did not make part of the musical system before; for the Greeks had gone no farther than the heptachord, or seven strings, till that time. This is the abridged substance of the account given by Nicomachus, in Harmon. Manual. p. 10; Gaudentius, in Harm. Introd. p. 13; Iamblichus, de Vit. Pythag. p. 97; Macrobius, in Somn. Scip. lib. 2. c. 1.

§ 13.
Objections.

Some difficulties occur to me in this story: 1st, If the weights were what all these writers mention, the sounds produced would not have been what they tell us. It is well known, that the weights must have been as the squares of those numbers. Yet all those who give this account agree as to the numbers; which error shews on what a precarious tradition this story was originally founded.

founded. 2dly, It seems very wonderful, and indeed incredible, that four hammers should be in the proportion requisite, by mere accident. 3. This story is not told by some of the best Greek writers, though they so frequently mention these celebrated numbers, and so frequently quote his doctrines in relation to music. 4thly, These very numbers were known to the Chaldæans, who, as Plutarch says, Vol. II. p. 1028, divided the seasons of the year by the fourth, fifth, and octave; making spring as 6; autumn as 8; winter as 9; and summer as 12. 5thly, But farther, Pythagoras could not find the numbers 6, 8, 9, 12, by the method above mentioned, without the help of a single string, which would have sufficed, without any weight at all: For though it is possible that he might observe that the numbers 36, 64, 81, 144, representing the weights necessary to produce the musical intervals, 4th, 5th, and 8th, supposed to be heard at the blacksmith's shop, were the squares of 6, 8, 9, 12; yet he certainly could not from thence conclude, that a single string, shortened in these proportions respectively, would give the same sounds; and therefore he must proceed thus.

Having prepared a string A B, fixed upon rests at each end, with a moveable bridge; such an one as Ptolemy used, and called a monochord; and having suspended weights, in the proportion of 36, 64, 81, 144, to four strings, he raises or lowers the tone of the string A B, till he finds it unison with string 36; next he stops somewhere in the string A B, till he finds an unison to the string 64; we will suppose the point found is E; he measures E B, and finds it to be ¾ of the whole string. Afterwards he stops somewhere in the string A B, till he finds an unison to string 81; we will suppose the point found is D; he measures D B, and finds it to be ⅔ of the whole string. Lastly, he does the same in regard to string 144, and finds the point C ½ of the whole string. Now call-

§ 14. *Discovery of intervals.* Fig. 2.

CHAP. I. ing A B 12, ¾ of 12 is 9, ⅔ of A B is 8, and ½ A B is 6. Here then we have the numbers that give the 4th, 5th, and 8th; but the same might have been done without the weights; for had he tuned several strings by the means of pegs; as is used on many instruments; or by the means of weights which he did not know adjusted, till the intervals became agreeable to the ear, he might, by making unisons with the several strings at several points on the single string, have found the proportions above-mentioned. If we suppose therefore the very reverse of this strange tale to have been the case, every thing will be natural: For it is highly probable, that so curious a man as Pythagoras might try what weights would produce the 4th, 5th, and octave; and he perhaps might be the first who ever made such an experiment. This was a sufficient ground for his ignorant admirers to build the whole story upon, without knowing the true numbers, or the impossibility of making out the intervals, without certain circumstances which they take no notice of. That Pythagoras did actually use this method, is probable, because he is said to have recommended the monochord to his disciples, Vide Aristid. p. 116.

§ 15.
Ptolemy.

The next considerable improvement made in music was filling up the octave, by Ptolemy the astronomer, in a way perfectly conformable to nature. He could not, I believe, prove it to be so; that task was left for Tartini, which he has done to a demonstration. Before the time of Ptolemy, there was no fixed rule for filling up the tetrachords: Some pretended to use two tones and a semitone, which intervals were settled by the ear only; for there is no such thing as a half tone, nor can be, in music: Others, as Pythagoras, and those who followed his doctrines, made use of two tones major, and a limma or remainder, represented by the proportion 243 : 256. This limma was arbitrary, as well as the two tones major, there being no two equal intervals following one

one another immediately in natural mufic. However the tone CHAP. I. major, confidered feparately, was perfectly right; for it was found by Pythagoras, upon meafuring the interval between the 4th and 5th. This gave him an advantage over the oppofite party, who neverthelefs continued to conteft the point, till Ptolemy's fyftem was known. From that time this fyftem was generally followed, till the temperament took place; and is ftill practifed by all fine players on the violin, violoncello, and fuch inftruments.

§ 16. Galileo.
From Ptolemy we muft make a great ftride, before we meet with any new difcovery; for the next was made by that excellent philofopher Galileo; who firft made ufe of the doctrine of pendulums to explain the principles of mufic, and, I believe, firft afcertained the law of the vibrations of pendulums in general. Vid. Difcorfi e Demonftrat. Matemat. p. 95, &c. He feems to have been extremely fond of mufic, and very defirous to account for the form of mufical ratios. He fays he had never met with any thing fatisfactory upon that fubject; and indeed nothing had appeared, as far as I know, that gave a phyfical folution of the pleafure we receive from mufic. Abftract numbers and proportions we meet with in abundance in every writer, both ancient and modern, upon this fubject; but abftract numbers and proportions are not phyfical caufes. Galileo was of this opinion, and therefore fought for fomething further; and having obferved that the times of the vibrations of pendulums are in the fubduplicate ratio of their lengths; fo that if you would have the time of the vibration of one pendulum to be double the time of the vibration of another pendulum, the length of the firft muft be four times the length of the laft; and alfo having obferved, that all the vibrations of the fame pendulum are performed in the fame time; he undertook from hence, and fome other phænomena, to deduce fuch principles of harmony, as, he fays, in part fatisfied

Chap. I. satisfied him. It is well known that he was mistaken, when he thought that all vibrations of the same pendulum are performed in the same time; but this error does not in the least affect his doctrine; because the vibrations of a pendulum in small arcs, and small vibrations in a musical string, are respectively isochronous. He then observes, that, if you strike a string on a harpsichord, it will put into motion, and cause to sound, not only another string, which is unison to it, but even the 8th and 5th; for the string that is struck begins and continues to vibrate all the time that its resonance is heard. These vibrations cause the air near the string to vibrate, and, gradually extending farther and farther, affect not only all the strings of the same instruments, but also of other instruments that are near. The unison string, being disposed to make its vibrations in the same time as the string struck, begins on the first impulse to move a little; and a 2d, 3d, 20th, &c. impulse succeeding, and all in periodical times, it receives at last the same tremor as the string struck; just as a pendulum, by repeatedly blowing upon it in a proper manner, may be put in motion.

§ 17.
Phænomenon on a glass.

That such vibrations are produced in the air, appears highly probable, from the regular undulations which he observed in water contained in a glass, upon rubbing it on the edge and making it sound. This is a phænomenon at present commonly known; but what he adds, I do not remember ever to have seen; *viz.* that if the tone happens to rise to an octave, every undulation will be divided into half; an accident, says he, that clearly proves the form of the octave to be 1 : 2.

§ 18.
Phænomenon on a harpsichord.

He observes farther, that these undulations in the air, produced by the string, cause not only the unison string to vibrate, but also any other body disposed to tremble; so that if you fix on the

the side of the instrument different bits of hair, or other flexible matter, you will see, upon sounding the strings of a harpsichord, sometimes one of these pieces, sometimes another, tremble, according as the string struck performs its vibrations in the same time; whereas the other pieces will not move at the sound of this string, nor will that piece give any sound on striking another string.

§ 19. *Phænomena on copper plates.* He mentions another curious phænomenon produced upon scraping copper, which tends to confirm his doctrine; but I shall pass it over at present, and proceed to the conclusion he draws from the phænomena above-mentioned; which is, that the immediate and proximate cause of the form of musical intervals is not the length of strings, nor the tension, nor the thickness; but the proportion of the numbers of vibrations and undulations of the air, which strikes upon the drum of the ear, and causes it to tremble in the same time. From hence he accounts for the effect of consonances and dissonances, in an easy and natural way; but, to avoid prolixity, I shall not mention it; and shall finish all I have to say, about the musical system of this excellent and inventive philosopher, with observing, that Dr. Smith does not express himself accurately, in saying that he (Galileo) called in question the truth of musical ratios; for he only says, that no physical explication had been given of them, which is a very different affair; nor has his difficulty any thing in common with that of Huygens, as is there supposed. Smith's Harmonic. p. 247.

§ 20. *Dr. Wallis.* I come now to one of the most important discoveries ever made in music; for which we are indebted partly to Dr. Wallis, and partly to two other Gentlemen of Oxford. I shall give an account of it in the very words of Dr. Wallis, taken out of the Philosophical

Chap. I. Philosophical Transactions, abridged by Lowthorp, Vol. I. p. 606.

§ 21.
Points of reft.

"It hath been long since observed, that if a viol-string or lute-string be touched with the bow or hand, another string, on the same or another instrument, not far from it, if an unison, or an octave, or the like, will at the same time tremble of its own accord. But I can now add, that not the whole of that other string doth thus tremble, but the several parts severally, according as they are unisons to the whole or the parts of that string so struck. For instance, supposing A B to be an upper octave to *a c*, and therefore an unison to each half of it stopped at *b*; if, while *a c* is open, A B be struck, the two halves of this other, i. e. *a b* and *b c* will both tremble, but not the middle point, at *b*; which will easily be observed, if a little bit of paper be lightly wrapt about the string *a c*, and removed successively from one end of the string to the other.

Fig. 4.

§ 22.
The same.

"In like manner, if A B be an upper 12th to *a d*, and consequently an unison to its three parts equally divided in *b, c*, if, *a d*, being open, A B be struck, its three parts, *a b, b c, c d*, will severally tremble, but not the points *b, c*. In like manner, if A B be a double octave to *a e*, the four quarters of this will tremble when that is struck, but not the points *b, c, d*. So if C D be a 5th to *a d*, and consequently each half of that stopped in E an unison of this stopped in *b e*, while that is struck, each part of this will tremble severally, but not the points *b c*; and while this is struck, each of that will tremble, but not the point E. The like will hold in lesser concords; but the less remarkably as the number of divisions increases.

§ 23.
The same.

"This was first of all (as I know of) discovered by Mr. Wil-
"liam

"liam Noble, M. A. of Merton college; and by him shewed to
"some of our musicians about three years since; and after him,
"by Mr. Thomas Pigot, A. B. of Wadham college, without
"knowing that Mr. Noble had discovered it before. I add this
"further, which I took notice of upon occasion of making trial
"of the other, that the same string as ac, being struck in the
"midst of (at) b, each part being unison to the other, will give no
"clear sound at all, but very confused; and not only so, which
"others have observed, that a string does not sound clear if struck
"in the midst, but also, if ad be struck at b or c, where one part
"is an octave to the other; and in like manner if ae be struck at
"b or d; the one part being a double octave to the other; and so
"if af be struck in c or d; the one part being a 5th to the other;
"and so in other like consonant divisions; but the less remarkable,
"as the number of divisions increaseth. This and the former I
"judge to depend upon one and the same cause; viz. the con-
"temporary vibrations of the several unison parts, which make
"one part tremble at the motion of the other; but when struck
"at the respective points of divisions, the sound is incongruous,
"by reason the point is disturbed, which should be at rest."
Philosophical Transactions, abridged by Lowthorp, Vol. I. p. 607.

In order of time, the discovery of the three sounds heard in § 24.
every musical string, when struck, which Monsʳ. Rameau attri- Rameau.
butes to Mersennus, should have been mentioned before; but I
reserved it for this place; where I am to observe, that the above-
mentioned skilful musician first applied this important discovery
to the purpose of practical music, and was thereby enabled to
reduce its rules into a clearer and shorter method, than had ever
been done before. But he fell into errors, a few of which I may
perhaps take notice of as I go along, for want of knowing
something farther, which Tartini has supplied.

It

CHAP. I.

§ 25.
Trumpet Marine.

It may perhaps seem extraordinary, that I have said nothing all this while about the discovery of the singular properties of the Trumpet Marine, though I took notice of its importance § 3. My reason for this omission was, that I am totally ignorant when, or by whom, this instrument was invented. I should imagine, that it was not known to the ancient musicians, as there is not the least notice taken of it amongst them, as far as I can find; and it does not seem probable that they should pass over in silence a phænomenon so very singular, if they were acquainted with it. On the other hand, the Greeks were certainly acquainted with the Common Trumpet, as early as the time of Homer; yet they never mention the defect of certain notes on that instrument, which are just the same as are wanting on the Trumpet Marine. But whether it was or was not known to the ancients is not a matter of any importance; that it should be known is of the greatest, as will appear before we proceed much farther. But to return to Tartini.

CHAP. II.

§ 26.
Of the circle and square.

I suppose there never was an artist of real genius, who was not solicitous to discover the principles upon which his art was founded. Tartini is a striking proof of this assertion, throughout his whole treatise, and particularly in this 2d chapter, of which I am now to give a very short account, and to me an unpleasing one. One cannot, without some impressions of compassion, see him wandering in the perplexing labyrinths of abstract ideas, almost without a guide, or at best with one which it is most likely would mislead him. He must have taken infinite pains to pursue nature in a wrong path, and trace her footsteps where she seems to have come by chance. He had fancied that harmony was to be found only in the circle, in conjunction with the square, which he looked upon as inseparable companions, and essentially united. They really proved in his hands, what they have been often called,
magical;

magical; for I can think it little less than magic, that he found **CHAP. II.** the mistress he was in pursuit of there, but with so few tokens of legitimacy about her, that a man must be little less than an enthusiast, or he would have suspected some deceit, had she not furnished proofs in her favour, of a nature totally foreign to what are required in such a case, and those confirmed him in his error.

§ 27. Ptolemy was deceived in the same manner exactly: He also firmly believed, as did all the antients, that no other figure but the circle was worthy of the heavenly bodies to move in: and though it is certain, that the heavenly bodies do not move in circles, yet by the help of geometry, and an ingenious system, he was able to solve the phænomena of the universe almost in every case. But, in some particulars, Kepler affords an example more resembling Tartini. He was, according to Maclaurin's account, all his life in pursuit of fancied analogies; in which Tartini also abounds; and we may apply to the latter, what he (Maclaurin) says of the former; that to this disposition we owe such discoveries as are more than sufficient to excuse his conceits. Account of Sir Isaac Newton, &c. p. 49.

Ptolemy's circles.

Kepler.

§ 28. What I have already said, will be a sufficient excuse for my not entering into a detail on this long chapter; as such a detail would be extremely tedious to some, unintelligible to others, and would appear strange to the only men, who are qualified to form any judgment on this matter, I mean the mathematicians. However, in order to vindicate the harshness of this censure, I will just mention one or two instances of his errors. 1st, he says, "that it is demonstrable by algebra, that unity, and an indeterminate quantity x being given, no other harmonic mean can be found between them but the number 2;" whereas it is demonstrable,

Tartini's errors.

CHAP. II. monstrable, both by algebra and the nature of the hyperbola, that 2 cannot be an harmonic mean between unity and any other number less than infinite. This would not suit his purpose. 2dly, He says upon this occasion, and others, that though there may be demonstration against him, yet his demonstration may be true, because he means quite another thing by his x, which he calls indefinite, than what mathematicians mean by their x, which they suppose infinite; and adds, that it is known amongst mathematicians, that this is not the only case, where two opposite propositions may be demonstratively proved.

§ 29.
Errors of another kind.

Fig. 4.

His other errors are quite of another kind, and, besides being curious as mere matters of speculation, have the merit of leading him right. I call them errors, because they are, as I observed before, arbitrarily pressed into the service of music; and not because the propositions themselves are false. I shall therefore lay them before the reader. In the circle ABM, fig. 4. let the diameter AM be divided according to the harmonic series, $\frac{1}{2}, \frac{1}{3}, \frac{1}{4}$, &c.; draw the chords AB, AC, AD, &c. and the ordinates $\frac{1}{2}$B, $\frac{1}{3}$C, $\frac{1}{4}$D, &c. and the complements to the chords MB, MC, MD, &c.; square the chords, and they will be $\frac{1}{2}, \frac{1}{3}, \frac{1}{4}$, &c. i. e. they will represent the harmonic notes in fig. 4, example 1 and 2. Square the chords supplement, and they will give $\frac{1}{2}, \frac{2}{3}, \frac{3}{4}$, &c. viz. the notes in example N° 3, which arise from the arithmetical division of a string, some of the very notes wanting to fill up the octave in common use. Lastly, square the ordinates $\frac{1}{2}$B, $\frac{1}{3}$C, $\frac{1}{4}$D, &c. and they will be $\frac{1}{4}, \frac{2}{9}, \frac{3}{16}$, &c. i. e. they will represent the notes in N° 4. example, which he calls discords; two of which certainly do not belong to the diatonic scale; the other three; viz. C, D, F, certainly do; and therefore cannot be called discords, according to his own principles.

It muſt appear a very ſingular thing, that moſt of all the notes commonly practiſed ſhould ariſe in a regular way from a figure which ſeems to have nothing in common with harmony, and thoſe too in their exact proportions. Who would not be ſtruck with ſuch a coincidence? but who would think of looking for muſical notes in ſuch a place? Yet why not? the circle has bewitched many a ſober man. Its great ſimplicity and beauty, joined to the facility of drawing it, naturally tempts every one to deduce from its properties whatever can be deduced, rather than from the properties of any figure; inſomuch that this is a ſtanding rule amongſt mathematicians. I have no doubt but if Tartini had been as well acquainted with the hyperbola as with the circle, and had the hyperbola been as eaſy to draw, he would have ſought for his ſyſtem rather there; becauſe it is actually in its own nature harmonical; and I verily believe, that, with his ſagacity and unwearied diligence, he would have found the ſame ſyſtem in that figure. But I muſt obſerve, that coincidences are often merely accidental; and therefore are no proof that we have found the true explication of any thing, becauſe we, in our reſearches meet with them: I gave an inſtance of the contrary already, in Ptolemy's aſtronomy. But, after all, how this coincidence ſhould happen will eaſily appear; for fig. 4. $\frac{1}{7} \times \frac{2}{7}$ equals A M or the diameter; i. e. as $\frac{1}{7}$ gives the harmonic note, $\frac{2}{7}$ or the ſupplement will give the correſpondent arithmetic note. But, by the known property of the circle, $AC^2 \times CM^2 = AM^2$; i. e. the ſquare of the chord, added to the ſquare of the ſupplement, equals the ſquare of the diameter; therefore, if the ſquare of the chord repreſents an harmonic, the ſquare of the ſupplement repreſents its correſpondent arithmetical note; for the whole ſquare repreſents the fundamental note: ſo

CHAP. II.

§ 30.

Lead to truth.

that

[20]

CHAP. II. that Tartini has only substituted surfaces in the room of lines. As to fines, I do not find any solution.

§ 31.
Spirit of system.

It may be asked, what occasion there was for Tartini's searching for the notes in N° 2. example, fig. 1, when he had them ready found to his hands, in the very step he took to search after them; for the diameter must be first divided into $\frac{1}{2}, \frac{1}{3}, \frac{1}{4}$, &c. i. e. harmonically, before he could apply the several parts, in order to find the chords. But the diameter is a right line, that might as well be the diameter of any other figure, as well as of the circle; and he wanted to deduce all from the circle. It may be natural therefore for some people to ask this question; but not for any man who ever felt the spirit of system working in him. Must some of Tartini's notes be deduced from the circle, and others from a right line? as well give up the whole, or better; for then all consistency, the chief merit, is gone. For this reason, he set out with endeavouring to prove the inseparability of the circle and square. Had he not done this, the inconsistency I just mentioned would, he foresaw, be objected to him.

§ 32.
Use of Tartini's discovery about the circle.
Fig. 4.

I do not know whether it be worth while to observe, that the first series, deduced in the manner Tartini has done, furnishes a method of making a square or circle any aliquot part of another square or circle, where the numerator is unity. For let A M, fig. 4, be the side of the given square, or A B M the circle; and let it be required to find another square or circle, which shall be to the given square as 1 : 3; draw the chord A C, and the square of it will be the side of a square equal to $\frac{1}{3}$ of the given square. The same may be done, if a square $\frac{1}{4}, \frac{1}{5}$, &c. of a given square is required. But if a square, which shall be $\frac{2}{3}, \frac{3}{4}$, &c. of another, is required, then draw M C, M D, &c. and do the same as before, i. e. take M C, M D, for the side of the square required.

The

The method of making a square, double, triple, &c. of a given square, is well known; but this problem, as far as I know, is quite new.

CHAP. II.

§ 33. *Drum.*

I have hitherto omitted to give an account of another phænomenon, mentioned by Tartini in this second chapter; it is curious, but whether new, I know not: " Let there be," fays he, " a fo-
" norous cylinder; for example, a drum; let it be beat; and
" if the two fkins be unifon, you will hear two founds; one na-
" tural to the inftrument, call it C; the other of confent, and
" will be G below, i. e. lower 4th to the natural found. Sepa-
" rate from the drum the upper or lower fkin, leaving the little
" circle on, which faftened it down, and kept it tight. When
" you beat now, you will hear two founds, as before; one will
" be the fame C, which is the natural found; but the other,
" which is the found of confent, will not any longer be G below,
" but G above, which is a 5th to the other found. The expe-
" riments muft be made with great exactnefs; the two fkins
" of the drum muft be unifon, equal, and as fmooth as poffible,
" that the effect may be evident." He draws confequences from this phænomenon, in favour of his fyftem; but fuch as, I believe, will hardly be admitted by mathematicians. For this reafon, I fhall pafs on.

§ 34. *Tartini's deduction, why right.*

I obferved above, § 28, that Tartini's deductions from the circle and fquare give the true fyftem of mufic; it may therefore be reafonable to afk me, how I can know this, when I look on his theory as imaginary, and all others as imperfect? To which I anfwer, that I know his deductions to be true by another theory, not liable, I believe, to any objection. This theory it fhall be my bufinefs to explain, in a fhort compafs, and in a way level to the capacity of almoft every reader. I chufe to explain it in this

place,

CHAP. II. place, and before I enter upon giving an account of the 3d chapter; becaufe there will begin matter of another fort, and which fuppofes, in general, a knowledge of the principles of mufic.

§ 35.
Trumpet Marine.
Fig. 5.

Inftead of referring to § 2 for an account of the phænomena of the monochord, I fhall, for the eafe of the reader, and alfo becaufe I have fome neceffary obfervations to make upon them, repeat the whole again in this place. Let the line K L, fig. 5. reprefent a mufical ftring, firmly fixed at each end, and ftretched properly. This ftring, when founded in the way I fhall defcribe, is called the Trumpet Marine: K C is $\frac{1}{2}$ of K L, K G $\frac{1}{3}$ of K L, K c $\frac{1}{4}$ of K L, K E $\frac{1}{5}$ of K L, K g $\frac{1}{6}$ of K L. Prefs the ftring gently and laterally at any of the points $\frac{1}{2}, \frac{1}{3}, \frac{1}{4}$, &c. with your finger, and ftrike the longer part of K L with a bow, and you will hear a mufical found, which found arifes from K G, K c, K E, &c. and not from G L, c L, E L, &c. the longer part. I have placed under every divifion the name by which every note is called by muficians.

§ 36.
Trumpet Marine.

I fhall now make an obfervation or two on the notes of this Trumpet Marine. 1ft then, the firft note that arifes after the octave $\frac{1}{2}$, is G $\frac{1}{3}$, or the octave and 5th above it, i. e. the 12th above the found of the whole ftring. The fecond note, c $\frac{1}{4}$, is 2 octaves above the whole ftring; and fo of the reft. This progreffion of founds is reprefented in fig. 1, examples 1 and 2. 2dly, No 4th or 6th can ever arife in this way; fo that it feems impoffible to fill up the octave in common ufe, without finding out fome other method; for we are not to take it for granted, that, becaufe mathematicians have contrived numbers for intervals, that therefore they ought to be adopted as a part of mufic intended by nature; if fo, many inconfiftencies and abfurdities would follow, in this and other arts. 3dly, I defire the reader

to recollect what I mentioned towards the beginning of this trea- CHAP. II.
tife, that no diſtinct ſound will be heard, upon ſtriking the monochord, unleſs the upper part be an aliquot part of the whole,
i. e. unleſs it meaſures the whole without a remainder. Now
this can never happen, unleſs the fraction that expreſſes the part
has unity for its denominator.

§ 37.
Theſe things being premiſed, let us proceed. Suppoſe now
this Trumpet Marine to be changed into a monochord, and to *Trumpet Marine and Monochord compared.*
be ſtopped on a finger board, or bridge, at the ſame point of
diviſion, $\frac{1}{2}, \frac{1}{3}, \frac{1}{4}$, &c. and let us ſee what will be the conſequence. In this caſe, if the longer part of the ſtring is ſtruck
with a bow, that part will ſound. Thus, if the ſtring is ſtop-
ped at $\frac{1}{3}$, then L $\frac{2}{3}$ will ſound; and ſince K $\frac{1}{2}$ is $\frac{1}{2}$ of the whole,
K L, L $\frac{2}{3}$, will be $\frac{3}{4}$; but $\frac{3}{4}$ repreſents a 5th above K L: Therefore the note is the very ſame that we found when the upper part
K $\frac{1}{3}$ gave the ſound. Let the ſtring now be ſtopped at $\frac{1}{4}$; then
$\frac{3}{4}$ L will ſound; and ſince K $\frac{1}{2}$ is $\frac{1}{2}$ of the whole ſtring, $\frac{3}{4}$ L will
be $\frac{3}{8}$ of the whole ſtring; but $\frac{3}{8}$ repreſents a fourth. Therefore
we have here a new note called F. Next, Let the ſtring be ſtopped
at $\frac{1}{5}$, then $\frac{4}{5}$ L will ſound; and ſince K $\frac{1}{2}$ is $\frac{1}{2}$ of the whole ſtring,
$\frac{4}{5}$ L will be $\frac{4}{5}$ of it; but $\frac{4}{5}$ repreſents a 3d major; therefore the
note is the ſame that was found when K $\frac{1}{5}$ gave the ſound.
Laſtly, Let the ſtring be ſtopped at $\frac{1}{6}$, and then $\frac{5}{6}$ L will give the
ſound; and ſince K $\frac{1}{2}$ is $\frac{1}{2}$ of the whole, $\frac{5}{6}$ L will be $\frac{5}{6}$ of it;
but $\frac{5}{6}$ repreſents a 3d minor, which is another new note. When
I ſay that L $\frac{1}{3}$, and $\frac{3}{4}$ L, give the ſame note as K G and K E,
I mean as to denomination; for octaves make no difference.

§ 38.
Upon theſe phænomena I ſhall make ſome obſervations. 1ſt
then, Theſe notes, contrary to the progreſſion of the harmonic *Monochord*
notes, deſcend, as may be ſeen fig. 3, examples 2 and 3; from *and String*
Trumpet.
whence

Chap. II. whence this confequence may be drawn, that the rule amongft muficians, that parts in concert fhould move contrary ways, is founded on nature. That they do defcend, is evident at firft fight; for juft in proportion as that part of the ftring is fhortened which produces the harmonic notes, it is lengthened in that part which produces the correfpondent notes in the common fcale. 2dly, This fcale is called the arithmetical; becaufe the new note F divides the octave arithmetically: For fuppofing C to be added below, it will be expreffed by the number 60, fig. 1, example 3. Now c 30 falls as much fhort of F 45, as F 45 does of 60. On the other hand, G 45, the other mean, divides the fame octave harmonically; for 30 is to 60 as the difference between 30 and 40 is to the difference between 40 and 60. So again, E^b 50 divides the 5th, G 40, c 60, arithmetically; whereas E 48 divides it harmonically, as will appear upon trial. The ufe of this laft obfervation will appear afterwards.

§ 39.
Monochord and String Trumpet.

Fig. 2.

My next ftep will be to fhew, that the notes in example 3. are naturally connected with the notes that ftand over them; and that the found of the whole ftring is the univerfal and fundamental bafe of them all, both in examples 2 and 3, fig. 1. In order to prove this, I muft refer to § 3, where it was afferted as a known fact, that when a ftring founds in the fhort part, it founds becaufe it is an aliquot part of the long part, as well as of the whole; therefore, when A $\frac{1}{4}$, (fig. 2.) founds, the whole ftring, as well as the longer part $\frac{3}{4}$ B, is divided into aliquot parts; i. e. this laft is divided into 3, viz. from $\frac{1}{4}$ to $\frac{1}{2}$, from $\frac{1}{2}$ to F, and from F to B, each of which is equal to A $\frac{1}{4}$, and vibrates, and confequently founds, however obfcurely, as well as the longer part, and the whole ftring. Now the longer part $\frac{3}{4}$ B is a 4th to the whole ftring, and is the very note found upon ftopping clofe at that point of divifion. I chofe this inftance to prove my affertion, for

an

an obvious reason; but any other instance would have served as well. Here then we have all the fundamental notes in music, *viz.* C, F, G, intimately and essentially connected together, and arising necessarily with the harmonic division. They are the same which Tartini deduces, with a most complicated apparatus, from various proportions, and groundless notions about the circle, and had they not been confirmed by the phænomenon of the 3d sounds, they must have remained of doubtful authority. In order to give the reader a clear conception how all these notes arise on the trumpet marine, I have exhibited them in fig. 6. N° 1 and 2. They both represent the same string. N° 1 has the notes arising from the shorter part of the trumpet marine; N° 2, those arising from the longer; and the curves represent the vibrations of the part: Thus, while K $\frac{1}{2}$ vibrates in N° 1, $\frac{1}{4}$ L vibrates in N° 2, &c.

CHAP. II.

Fig. 6.

It will be said, perhaps, that, according to the foregoing doctrine, it is not enough that each note should make an aliquot part of the whole, but that each interval should be an aliquot part or parts of every other interval; or, what comes to the same, that the intermediate spaces between the notes should be an aliquot part or parts of every interval, v. g. the spaces fig. 6. N° 1. between $\frac{1}{6}$ and $\frac{1}{5}$, $\frac{1}{5}$ and $\frac{1}{4}$, &c. Let us then examine how this is in fact: If $\frac{1}{5}$ be deducted from $\frac{1}{4}$, there remains $\frac{1}{20}$ of the whole string; if $\frac{1}{6}$ be deducted from $\frac{1}{4}$, there remains $\frac{2}{24}$, or $\frac{1}{12}$, or $\frac{3}{60}$; if $\frac{1}{6}$ be deducted from $\frac{1}{5}$, there remains $\frac{1}{30}$, or $\frac{2}{60}$; if $\frac{1}{6}$ be deducted from $\frac{1}{4}$, there remains $\frac{1}{2}$, or $\frac{30}{60}$. Again, if $\frac{1}{5}$ be deducted from $\frac{1}{4}$, there remains $\frac{1}{20}$, or $\frac{3}{60}$; if $\frac{1}{5}$ be deducted from $\frac{1}{3}$, there remains $\frac{2}{15}$, or $\frac{8}{60}$; if $\frac{1}{5}$ be deducted from $\frac{1}{2}$, there remains $\frac{3}{10}$, or $\frac{18}{60}$. Again, if $\frac{1}{4}$ be deducted from $\frac{1}{3}$, there remains $\frac{1}{12}$, or $\frac{5}{60}$; if $\frac{1}{4}$ be deducted from $\frac{1}{2}$, there remains $\frac{2}{7}$, or $\frac{1}{4}$, or $\frac{15}{60}$. Lastly, if $\frac{1}{3}$ be deducted from $\frac{1}{2}$, there remains $\frac{1}{6}$, or $\frac{10}{60}$. Hence it appears, that all the intermediate spaces between the notes may break into aliquot parts when they vibrate,

§ 40. *Objection:*

E and

CHAP. II. and that the smallest vibrating part is $\frac{1}{60}$ of the whole string; and supposing the whole string be one foot long, the smallest vibrating part will be no more than $\frac{1}{5}$ of an inch long. That so small a part should vibrate seems to us almost incredible, but nothing ought to be esteemed really so, which is deduced by just reasoning from certain and notorious facts. Thus far all the notes are harmonious; let us step out of the hexachord, and see what will be the case. Deduct $\frac{1}{5}$ from $\frac{1}{6}$, and there remains $\frac{1}{72}$, which does not divide 60, and therefore has no common measure with any of the notes in the hexachord. The same may be said of almost all the rest. I have many observations to make on the foregoing doctrine; but as my whole system is not yet compleatly explained, I shall defer them for the present; and endeavour to set this affair in the clearest light I am able, by removing some apparent difficulties.

§ 41.
Trumpet Marine and Musical string.

First, then, the common phænomenon of the Trumpet Marine, § 3, proves, that if an aliquot part of a string is sounded, the longer part, as well as the whole, sounds likewise; for if it be touched in any point but that which makes the shorter part an aliquot of the whole, no distinct sound is heard, but a jarring noise is produced. Now this could not happen, if the longer part did not also sound, and by this means produce the jarring above-mentioned. 2dly, That it is possible for the longer part, as well as the whole, to sound in their respective totalities, is evident by the phænomenon mentioned § 2. viz. that, when a musical string is sounded, the 3d and 5th, or rather the 17th and 12th, are heard along with the sound of the whole string. 3dly, The experiment mentioned by Dr. Wallis, vide § 20, proves the same point. 4thly, The phænomenon of the 3d sounds, discovered by Tartini, confirms the whole. Here then is a coincidence of experiments that mutually support one another, and must remove all doubts concerning the proposition laid down in § 39,

that

that the notes in example 3, fig. 1, are naturally connected with CHAP. II. thofe notes over them in example 2; and the note of the whole ſtring is the univerſal and fundamental baſe of them all.

But it will be faid, that there remains behind, example 4. fig. 1. § 42. of which I have given no account. This contains the difcords; *Objection.* and it will perhaps be thought impoſſible to deduce thefe, without uſing his propofitions, or fomething analogous to them. If this is impoſſible, then my fyftem is incompleat; for thefe difcords, and many others, are allowed by all profeſſors to be extremely agreeable, and are certainly neceſſary, according to the modern taſte. Befides, one of thofe notes is wanted to fill up the diatonic fcale; viz. D; which by no means can be found in the way I found the other notes. This difficulty muſt be removed, and ſhall be, in the next chapter, to which we are now coming; but I will firſt give an account of a curious phænomenon mentioned in it.

Towards the beginning of the third chapter, Tartini gives CHAP. III. a propofition which he takes to be new, and I believe is ſo: It is this; that if weights, as 1, 2, 3, 4, &c. be fufpended § 43. by ſtrings of the fame diameter, but in length, as A M, *Strings with* A B, A C, A D, &c. i. e. the diameter and chords of the *weights as* circle anſwering to the points $\frac{1}{2}$, $\frac{1}{3}$, $\frac{1}{4}$, &c. fig. 4. thefe ſtrings, *1, 2, 3.* when founded, will give the harmonic notes. This I take to be his meaning; for it is not a little obſcure. As I do not underſtand his proof, I will give one of my own. It is a known thing, and mentioned before, that ſtrings equal in length, with weights as 1, 4, 9, 16, &c. will give founds as 1, $\frac{1}{2}$, $\frac{1}{3}$, $\frac{1}{4}$, &c. Now 2 is a mean between 1 and 4, 3 is a mean between 1 and 9, 4 is a mean between 1 and 16, &c. But A B is a mean between A M and A $\frac{1}{2}$, A C is a mean between A M and A $\frac{1}{3}$, A D

Chap. III. is a mean between A M and A ¼, &c. Therefore strings of the lengths A M, A B, A C, A D, &c. with weights as 1, 2, 3, 4, &c. will give the same sounds as strings of the length A M, with weights as 1, 4, 9, 16, &c.; for mean weights with mean lengths must have the same effects as extreme weights with extreme lengths, respectively.

§ 44.
Third minor.
After many numerical calculations, which I shall pass over entirely, Tartini undertakes to account for the system of the third minor, that greatest of all difficulties in harmony, and to shew its necessary connection with the system of the third major, to which he has added a difficulty that was not known before; for he found, that upon sounding some chords in the third minor, p. 67, that the 3d sounds, which were double, were intolerable; and so they appeared to eight professors, who were present when the experiment was made; whereas the same chords in the third major were perfectly agreeable, producing only single third sounds. From hence he concludes, that if the third sounds could be heard as distinctly as the natural sounds, the execution of music would be impossible, in the system of the third minor. But I shall not enter upon this subject, i. e. the system of the third minor, at present, as a better opportunity of considering it will occur afterwards.

§ 45.
Discords.
He proceeds to the examination of dissonances and discordances, and their preparation and resolution. The notes in example 4, fig. 1, he calls dissonances; those in example 3, fig. 1, discordances. The reason he gives for this distinction is, that the dissonances require both preparation and resolution; the discordances only resolution. He then enters into particulars, and shews the manner of preparing and resolving the 4th, the 6th, the 7th, and 9th; as for the 2d, he rejects it, and proves it to be

no

no discord, explaining clearly how the mistake happened, viz. by an inversion of the harmony, p. 66. He also clears up the dispute about the 4th, and shews that it arose by confounding that 4th which belongs to the trumpet marine with that which belongs to the monochord; and lastly adds a new discord, which he calls the superfluous 13th, and resolves in a new way. Before him, all discords, he says, were resolved upon the first and second base only; this discord is resolved on the third base, i. e. G✷ descends to G, which is third base to C. For farther particulars, I shall refer the reader, who is curious in these matters, to the original, which, I am certain, he will find well worthy of his perusal; and come to what I promised, § 42, about the discords.

CHAP. III.

The method I take to find the discords is as follows: Let us take any of the notes in example 3, fig. 1. for a base, which must be allowable, as they have all been proved to be connected with the harmonic notes that stand over them; and let us see what will be the consequence, according to phænomenon § 2. Let the note be G, which sounded, will give 3d and 5th as harmonic notes. Here then we have not only got D, but B also, which was wanting to fill up the diatonic scale, &c. and though a discord does not appear in any of the scales fig. 1. Next let F be made the base, which will produce A and C; A was wanting in all the scales. Again, take E for a base; this will produce G✷ and B. G✷ is a new note, and the very same with that in example 4, fig. 1; for the interval from G to G✷ is 24 : 25, as Tartini makes it. Lastly, take E^b for a base, and it will produce G and B^b; this last is a new note, and the same with that in example 4, fig. 1.

§ 46. *Invention of discords.*

I pretend not to any merit in using this method of finding the discords; it is the very same that Tartini himself takes to fill up the diatonic scale, as will appear afterwards. Why he did not pursue

§ 47. *Tartini misled as to discords.*

Chap. III. pursue it, in order to find all the discords, I cannot guess, unless because he was misled by his fondness for the square and circle; which can be the only reason why he has omitted B in his scale of discords, though he calls it a discord, and shews the different ways of resolving it; for I suppose he could not possibly find it in his favourite figures. Though I speak thus freely of Tartini, I mean not to set myself in competition with that truly great artist, not even as to theory: On the contrary, had he not traced out the whole system as he has done, and pointed out the way in every step I have taken, and shall take, throughout this treatise, I should never have been able to prove, in a method much more simple, and I imagine more convincing, what he undertook to prove with infinite pains; and, I must add, with some perplexity. Mere accident indeed led me at first, having a curiosity to see what notes the longer part of a string, if stopped as on a violin, at each division of the harmonic intervals, would produce; but without his assistance I should have been totally incapable of making the use I have done, and shall do, of this scale.

§ 48.
Resolution of discords.

Not only my method of finding the discords, but my idea of them, and of their resolution, is different from that of Tartini: It is taken however from his examples, though not from his doctrine. My idea then of a dissonance is, that if two consonant notes be held on, while a third note changes to another harmony, the two notes, which were pleasing before, become disagreeable, if not resolved, because they do not belong to it. All the instances Tartini gives of dissonances and discordances, p. 80, 81, are of this sort. From hence it appears, that all chords commonly called dissonant, are such by position only, and consequently every note may be rendered dissonant; but to do it properly is the work of skill and genius only. In fact, there can possibly be no consonance but with the harmonic notes, and therefore

therefore all chords muſt take their origin from thence, and end CHAP. III.
there. But beſides the method of introducing diſcords, by continuing two notes while the third changes to another harmony, diſcords may be introduced, by taking in a note before its time, that belongs to another; however this comes to the ſame. Theſe two caſes, and the inverſion of notes, will, I believe, account for all the figures properly placed over baſe notes, for the harpſichord. As to the 7th, I ſhall conſider it in another place.

§ 49.
Errors about diſcords.

If the foregoing doctrine about diſſonances is juſt, then, 1ſt, what Dr. Smith aſſerts, in his Harmonics, That nature has put no limits between them and conſonances, is not true; but it is a common error to conſider intervals per ſe, and not in relation to a ſyſtem, as Tartini obſerves, and has given an inſtance in two parts, where the 5ths are conſonant, and by adding a baſe to them they became diſſonant. 2dly, It is ſaid in the Harmonics, that there is no harmony without diſcords. This is not ſtrictly true; for there are none, as long as we confine ourſelves to the notes on the ſtring trumpet, i. e. in all tunes properly compoſed for the trumpet and German horn; though there are both the 6ths, the 4th, and both the 3ds, on that inſtrument. But the propoſition is true, as ſoon as we uſe the diatonic ſcale; for there all muſic conſiſts in a perpetual reſolution of imperfect conſonances and real diſſonances.

§ 50.
Apology for ſhortneſs.

What I have ſaid upon the ſubject of diſſonances, and their reſolution, will appear very ſhort and imperfect, to all ſuch readers as are converſant in the practical part of muſic; but, I think, the ſhortneſs ought not to be deemed as an objection, if there is no deficiency; I mean, as to the principles which I have uſed; as to the practice, I know too well the perplexity and intricacy of this part of muſic, to pretend to give any inſtructions; and

were

CHAP. III. were I able and inclined to do so, it would be unnecessary, as Tartini has done it already to my hands. I might indeed have translated this part of his work, as I have done some others, and as I might have translated the whole; but that did not suit my purpose. I shall therefore put an end to my observations on the third chapter.

CHAP. IV.

§ 51.
Octave.

Chapter the 4th contains many curious and instructive observations, of which I shall give some account in my usual way, adding, as I go along, reflections of my own. Our author sets out with a principle, which he had mentioned in the last chapter, that harmony must be supposed, before the parts which arise from the harmony, i. e. the song. The difference between them is this; in the harmony, the sounds are simultaneous; in the song, they are successive. These successive notes constitute the octave, and therefore it is of great consequence to settle this. I believe most people will be apt to think, that there was not much thought required to settle the common octave, which almost every one who has an ear can run over with the greatest ease, and, as he thinks, naturally; yet there were many divisions of it proposed, before that was invented which now takes place. Ptolemy the astronomer was the inventor; and it is no wonder it has generally prevailed from his time to this day, as it is the only one which was truly founded on nature. However this foundation does not appear by any thing we find in Ptolemy; nor does it appear in any other writer, but Tartini, that I know of.

§ 52.
Octave.

When we first begin to learn music, we are, or should be, taught to play or sing the octave: Tartini used really to teach it, and sometimes to the great mortification of his conceited scholars; but he does not call it the foundation of music, as other masters do, who do not teach it. However, we are taught to go through

through it after a manner, and are ever after apt to look upon it as natural; but it is undoubtedly artificial, and the result of much and profound thought. However paradoxical therefore it may seem, yet it is certainly true, that harmony is more natural than the notes of the octave; for a string cannot be sounded, either as a trumpet marine, or as a monochord, i. e. in the common way, without producing harmony; whereas the notes of an octave never appear but in highly civilised countries. Amongst the birds we hear the 5th, the 4th, the 3d major and minor; but the notes of the octave from no animal that has not been taught, unless we believe the extraordinary account of the Sloth. The intervals we do hear, are those of every musical string, and therefore must be deemed natural.

CHAP. IV.

I have in part anticipated Tartini's method of getting the notes of the octave; but I will nevertheless repeat again what I said about it § 46. In order to obtain these notes, he takes the four notes which are expressed by the numbers 6, 8, 9, 12, or rather three of them, C, F, G; for the octave to C gives no new note; and then considers what other notes they will produce, according to the phænomenon of the musical string. He finds that C gives E and G; F gives A and C; and lastly, G gives B and D. But these notes fill up the diatonic scale or octave, and are exactly in the same proportions that Ptolemy first invented, and that have been in use ever since. From hence Tartini justly concludes, that the scale arises from the harmony, and not the harmony from the scale. This makes a great difference; and we shall see presently, that the want of this distinction has brought much confusion into music.

§ 53.
Octave.

But some will say, why pitch upon these three notes to fill up the octave, one of which does not even belong to the harmonic series,

§ 54.
Objection.

Chap. IV. series, viz. F; and particularly when the discords § 46 are produced in the same way, and yet do not belong to the common
scale? Is not this arbitrary? An answer to these objections must
Solution. be made. 1st then, All music consists in closes; and these closes
must be by rising a 4th, or, which comes to the same thing, by
falling a 5th. If it be asked, Why this must be? I answer, Because the ear requires it. Farther than this, I pretend not to go.
Taking it therefore for granted, as a principle, that in closing we
must rise a 4th, I shall proceed. There is no close in the harmonic notes but from G to C; and the next note that offers itself
naturally out of that series is F, being intimately connected with
G, as has already appeared, and will appear more strongly afterwards. However the ancients hit upon it, I do not pretend to
explain; but most certainly they adopted it very early, and laid
such a stress upon the invention, that the numbers which expressed
the two tetrachords became famous above all others. As to the
other part of the objection, that Tartini has proceeded in an arbitrary manner; I ask, whether that which is founded on a coincidence of physical causes, human sentiment, and mathematical
calculation, can be called arbitrary? Now this is the case of the
notes of the diatonic scale; and thus one of the finest arts is built
on the most solid foundation; an art that was undoubtedly first
begun in Ægypt, and from thence propagated over the rest of
the world, wherever any true music has been known!

§ 55. But why all this trouble, some musicians will say, to settle
Temperament. the notes of the scale, when it is notorious that they must all be
changed, upon the harpsichord, except the interval of the octave,
which alone can be perfectly in tune? Tartini observes, and very
truly, that singers and players conform to that instrument. He
then shews the necessity of this alteration of the true musical intervals, or, as it is called, the temperament; and subjoins what

I shall

I shall translate, for the benefit of the lovers of real harmony. CHAP. IV.

"Therefore it is necessary to increase the 3ds major, that they
"may fill up the octave; and diminish the 3ds minor, that
"they may not exceed the octave. The worst is, that this tem-
"perament has no certain laws. Some will have it equal through-
"out; some temper more, some less strongly; lastly, others
"more in one place than in another. This is so true, that in
"Italy, and other countries, much study is employed to find out
"a reasonable temperament, in which all nations may agree,
"(which is not the case at present,) where this music and these
"instruments are in use. But the case is desperate; because
"there is no room for a temperament in the form of proportions
"that arise from a system; and to pretend to deform ratios
"with reason, is a manifest contradiction. This affair stands
"more in need of prudence than of any thing else; and I infi-
"nitely applaud the opinion of P. Vallotti, our organ-master, as
"the most reasonable of all. He says, that you ought to give
"to the white keys of the organ all their natural perfection; both
"because they are the natural notes of the diatonic genus, and
"because in church-music the greatest use is made of them;
"throwing thus the greatest imperfection upon those black keys,
"which are most remote from the diatonic scale, and which are
"hardly ever used. Besides, he observes what pleasure results
"in playing on the organ (and he was a most excellent player,
"as he is now a most excellent composer, and thorough master
"of his art) from the contrast of the greater and less perfection
"of the chords, according as different modulations occur. If
"the temperament was equal, or a little more, a little less, in
"different places, there would not be that chiaro oscuro, which
"in practice produces a fine effect. This is the light in which
"he considers the temperament, and, in my judgment, so rightly,
"that there is no reasonable answer to be made. As for myself,

F 2 "as

CHAP. IV. " as my inftrument is the violin; on which when I play double
" ftops, I can hit upon the very form itfelf of the interval, the
" fign of which is, the 3d found, which ought to refult from
" the interval; I have the advantage, for myfelf and my fcho-
" lars, of a fure intonation, and confequently of the real ufe of
" the above-mentioned fcale, with all the precifion of the true
" ratios."

§ 56.

Imperfection of D F.

He next proceeds to obferve, that this fcale, though regularly deduced, is not entirely perfect in every poffible relation of the mufical notes that compofe it. He proves what is well known; and is moft certain, that D F falls fhort of a third minor, in the proportion of 80 : 81. " As for myfelf," fays he, " I leave the
" deficiency where nature has placed it, without thinking of di-
" viding it; and only obferve, that this imperfection arifes from
" the third minor, not in general, but fpecifically from that
" which depends on F, which is an arithmetical mean of the
" octave." This deficiency of D F makes the famous mufical

Comma.

comma, which has caufed fo much diffenfion amongft thofe who have written on mufic; for it is this very deficiency that gave rife to the temperament; and the temperament has given rife to many treatifes filled with fcience and ingenuity. Salinas, Zarlino, Huygens, Rameau, Euler, Smith, have all written upon this fubject; all able men; each of whom had his fyftem, and each has followers; but which fyftem is beft, is not yet determined. Yet, however they may difagree with one another in bringing this arduous matter about, they all agree to disfigure the fair form of harmony.

§ 57.

Solution.

But to return, and confider D F more particularly. Huygens, I believe, was the firft writer on mufic who obferved, that if we fing the notes C, F, D, G, C by perfect intervals, that the laft C will

C will be lower than the firſt C by a whole comma. His obſervation is undoubtedly true; but his concluſion from thence, that the voice therefore uſes a temperament, cannot be allowed of; for to uſe a temperament, is to deviate from the true proportions required by nature: Now here the proportion 32 : 27, which repreſents the interval D F, is fixed by nature; for F is a 4th to C, and a note of the hexachord, and therefore neceſſarily ſettled; and D is a 5th of the harmony we are going into, and therefore as neceſſarily ſettled. From whence it follows, that the interval D F, pro hic et nunc, is juſt what it ought to be. The truth is, that too much ſtreſs has been laid, by writers on muſic, on the leſſer intervals, and too little on the greater, as will appear afterwards.

CHAP. IV.

§ 58. *Solution continued.*

But I will go a ſtep farther, and obſerve, that D is in this place a diſcord, as every note taken out of the limits of the hexachord, and uſed as a baſe, muſt neceſſarily be. If it be ſhewn, therefore, that D is reſolved as all other diſcords are, nothing more is required, to put an end at once to all the difficulty about this famous paſſage: To ſhew this is very eaſy, by putting the harmony to F, D, and G; vide fig. 7; where F, A are held on, and D added, which becomes in the next chord part of the regular harmony of G. So much for the famous Comma, mentioned in that excellent book, intitled " Coſmotheorus," full of philoſophical imagination; which I ſhall have occaſion to cite, more than once, in the courſe of this work.

§ 59. *Harpſichord.*

I muſt obſerve, that though the deficiency in D F requires no temperament, as appears to me, while we remain in the principal tone G; yet, as ſoon as ever we go into another tone, either a temperament or a new note is required; v. g. you cannot make a full cloſe in G, 5th of C, with the notes only of the common ſcale;

for

Chap. IV. for D A will make an imperfect 5th. From hence it follows, that notes on open strings cannot be properly used on the violin in many cases; as indeed they are avoided, when neceffary, by all good players on that inftrument: For four ftrings, tuned perfect 5ths, following neceffarily, produce imperfect intervals. I prefume not to add any thing to what Tartini has faid about the harpfichord, as I know no remedy for its imperfections; palliating is all that can be thought of, and perhaps the method of doing it now in practice may be as good as any other. Like fome other fine machines, highly wrought up by art, in order to afford variety of entertainment, it is entitled to indulgence, and muft not be examined by too critical an infpection. Inftead of doing this, I will venture to fay fomething about a more homely inftrument, which was formerly the favourite of our anceftors, and is ftill the delight of our refpectable neighbours the Ancient Britons: Every one will immediately fee that I mean the Harp.

§ 60.
Harp.

As it is the common method to tune the Harp on any change of the key, this inftrument is capable of great perfection, and therefore deferves to be confidered. Without knowing certainly the ufual method of tuning, I will propofe one of my own, which perhaps may be new; and was, upon trial, approved of by a very good mafter on that inftrument. My method is as follows: From C to G, from G to D, perfect 5ths upwards; from C to F, a perfect 5th downwards; from F to A, a perfect 3d major; from A to E, and from E to B, perfect 5ths upwards. Thus we have C, D, E, F, G, A, B. i. e. all the natural notes in the common fcale; for the flats and fharps, make from B to F*, and from D to A, perfect 5ths; and we fhall have a perfect clofe in the key of G, as 5th of the principal C; and a tune for the Harp ought to wander no farther. However, the reft of the half-notes, as they are called, may be tuned according to the rule mentioned

§ 55.

§ 55. N. B. A ought to have a particular mark, when ufed in Chap. IV.
the key of G. As to tuning the Harp for the 3d minor, that
muft be confidered after that fyftem is fettled. It muft be obferved further, that if the key was to be changed from C to F,
it would not be fufficient, for accurate tuning, to make B flat,
and keep all the other notes as they ftood in C; as will appear
by comparing the two fcales together:

C $\frac{8}{9}$ D $\frac{9}{10}$ E $\frac{15}{16}$ F $\frac{8}{9}$ G $\frac{9}{10}$ A $\frac{8}{9}$ B $\frac{15}{16}$ C.

F $\frac{8}{9}$ G $\frac{9}{10}$ A $\frac{15}{16}$ B♭ $\frac{8}{9}$ C $\frac{8}{9}$ D $\frac{9}{10}$ E $\frac{15}{16}$ F.

Here the order of the notes is difturbed; for from C to D, in
the lower fcale, ought to be $\frac{9}{10}$, whereas it is $\frac{8}{9}$. But it is eafily
remedied: Only make from B♭ to D a perfect 3d major. The
fame may be done in any other fimilar cafe, i. e. when a new half
note is introduced, make the 3d to it perfect, and all the other
notes may ftand. This was done in order to tune for G, as
above defcribed.

§ 61. By this way of tuning, all the notes will be perfect in two
Harp. keys, on the Harp. Perfection, in all changes of the keys, cannot be had but with the voice, or on inftruments that can be
ftopped any where ad libitum; and even on thefe inftruments perfection cannot be had in fome cafes, where chords are played.
The advantage in this way of tuning is, not only that the intervals are more perfect than in any other way, but alfo, that there
will be a refonance in moft of the ftrings, which can never happen when any temperament is ufed. Had we compofitions made
purpofely for the Harp, of equal tafte with what are to be
found for fome other inftruments, this inftrument might pof-
fibly come once more into vogue, and pleafe the niceft ear,
that can bear fimplicity; but fuch compofitions are fcarcely to
be found.

To

CHAP. IV.
§ 62.
Harp.

To confirm what I faid above, § 59, that the Harp was formerly a favourite inftrument in this nation, I will cite fome paffages out of our old and beft writers.

" Mufic which his [Arion's] *Harp* did make."
Spenfer, Sonnet 38.

" Orpheus with his *Harp*." Ibid. Sonnet 44.

" By the judgment of Alcibiades, the *Harp* is to be preferred," &c. Praife of Mufic, printed 1586, p. 13.

" The *Harp* lived after Orpheus was dead." Ibid. p. 15. And in many other places *Harp* for Lyre.

" The office of a phyfician is to put the curious *Harp* of
" man's body in tune." Bacon, de Augm. Scien.

" His word is more than the miraculous *Harp*." Shakefpear's Tempeft, Act 2, fcene 1.

" The battle of the Centaurs, to be fung by an Athenian eu-
" nuch to the *Harp*." Midfummer Night's Dream, Act 5, fcene 1.

" *Harping* loud in folemn choir." Milton, on the Nativity, Stan. 11.

" And fet my *Harp* to notes of faddeft woe." Id. on the Paffion, Stan. 2.

" Touch their immortal *Harps* of golden wire." Id. at a folemn mufic.

" Then crown'd again, their golden *Harps* they took,

" *Harps* ever tun'd." Parad. Loft, B. 3. v. 365.

" And touch'd their golden *Harps*." B. 7. v. 258.

" And the found
" Symphonious of ten thoufand *Harps*, that tun'd
" Angelic harmony." Ib. v. 559.

" The *Harp* had work,
" And refted not." Ib. v. 594.

" A golden

"A golden *Harp* with silver strings she bore."
Cowley's Complaint.

CHAP. IV.

I have quoted no passage from Scripture on this occasion, because David's *Harp* is so well known, and the places, which are many, where that instrument is mentioned, are so familiar to every one; instead therefore of useless quotations from thence, I will just observe, that the word in the Septuagint, answering to *Harp* in our translation, is mostly Κιθαρα, but sometimes Ψαλτηριον, Κινυρα, or Ναβλα. All these instruments are essentially of the same nature, consisting of one row of strings without a finger-board; some were struck with the finger, others with a plectrum, and others perhaps with a stick, as our dulcimer. Prints of all these instruments are given by Monsignore Bianchini, in a book intitled, De Tribus Generibus Instrument. &c. from ancient monuments. Two of them, tab. 3, fig. 13 and 15, resemble in some degree the common Harp in shape: The first is taken from an Ægyptian vase in the villa Medici; the other from an ancient vase, belonging also to the Medici family, and has 12 strings, and therefore agrees with the Nablium of Josephus, as Bianchini observes. He also observes, that the Harp of the barbarians, mentioned by Venantius Fortunatus, in this line,

§ 63.
Lyre.

Romanusque lyrâ plaudat tibi, barbarus harpâ,

is properly compared with the Lyre. No doubt, these instruments are properly compared; for there seems to be no difference between them but a little in shape, and the number of strings, some of which were added after music had fallen from its ancient simplicity. I will add, that Bianchini finds, what he takes to be a Cithara, or Lyre, on a tripod placed before the bull Apis, in the Isiac table; which conjecture seems not improbable; this figure resembles the Harp. Diodor. Sic. p. 313, says expressly, that the instrument used by the bards was like the Lyre. From

CHAP. IV. all thefe circumftances, there is great reafon to think, that David's Nablium did not differ from the Old Britifh Harp with a fingle row of ftrings.

§ 64.
Cithara.

When I faid above, that the Κιθαρα, Ψαλτηριον, &c. were effentially of the fame nature, I went on the fuppofition, that the Cithara and Lyre did not differ, as Bianchini feems to fuppofe. It is true, thofe two words are frequently confounded, even by ancient writers; but Plato, p. 618, plainly makes a diftinction between them: What the difference was, does not appear, as far as I know. There is a mufical inftrument in Bianchini, found on an antique vafe, tab. 4, fig. 7, which is totally different from what is generally called the Lyre, fuch as is frequently found in the hands of Apollo, the Mufes, &c. It has a finger-board, and therefore moft undoubtedly was ftopped in playing, as the lute. This, Bianchini calls a Lyre, or Cithara; but the fame word cannot properly and critically be applied to two inftruments fo totally unlike. I fhould be inclined to call this the Cithara; and the more fo, as the words Guitar and Cithern feem to be derived from it. What Ariftotle fays of the Cithara feems to confirm all I have advanced; for he difapproves of it as an inftrument to be ufed in education, as being too artificial. This agrees very well to the Cithara, in contradiftinction from the Lyre, which was vaftly more fimple. I will farther obferve, that there feems to be a difference between the Lyras, properly fo called, in one refpect; for fome have a belly, or founding-board, others not.

§ 65.
Perfect mufic.

I faid, § 56, that to ufe a temperament is to disfigure the fair form of harmony; and will now add, that they only know what true harmony means, who have heard a well-compofed piece performed by a fet of muficians, who keep perfectly in tune with one another. I never heard fuch mufic but once, and
the

the effect was wonderful: It was performed in the Pope's chapel, during Paffion-week: It feemed to come from one fingle voice, and that the chords were only the refonances naturally belonging to it; or rather, the mufic did not feem to be produced by any human voice or inftrument; but that fpirits were diverting themfelves, and trying, like Ariel in the Tempeft, the powers of harmony over the human frame. It may be looked upon as whimfical, but I will venture to fay, that he who has not heard fuch mufic as I have defcribed, may get a better idea of it, by liftening to Æolus's Harp, than by any other way I can think of. Could we but add air and time to it, it would be the moft perfect of all mufical inftruments. But of this more in another place.

§ 66. *Harmonic notes.*

The refonances which I mentioned above, and by which I mean the harmonic notes, that conftantly accompany the found of every mufical ftring, are the life of mufic. Without thefe refonances, every found is flat and obfcure; and in a certain degree of this deficiency becomes mere noife; a ftring, that is not perfectly even throughout, gives an idea of what I have been faying. When we fay, by way of encomium, that a voice rings like a bell, we mean to exprefs that effect, which arifes from the harmonic notes; and probably the want of thefe notes is owing to fomething analogous to what I mentioned of a ftring, i. e. the organs that ferve for finging or fpeaking are not perfectly even or homogeneous throughout. Drawing a good tone out of a violin, I believe, depends not fo much upon any particular fleight, as fome people are apt to imagine, as on the following circumftances: 1ft, Having perfectly good and even ftrings; 2dly, Stopping perfectly well in tune; 3dly, and confequently, Not ufing open ftrings on certain occafions, where they muft be out of tune; 4thly, Striking at a proper diftance from the bridge, fo as not to interrupt

Chap. IV. the vibrations; vide § 23: All thefe circumftances are neceffary, in order to produce the refonances of which I have been fpeaking; but are too frequently neglected by muficians. I do not however exclude a certain fleight in managing the bow, which fome can never acquire, and which perhaps cannot be taught by the beft mafter. Thefe refonances give to mufic that identity and diverfity mentioned by Tartini; whereby every part is intimately fympathetic with every other part, and alfo with the whole. From hence it appears, that the word harmony has been with propriety employed to exprefs perfection, in many other fubjects, where identity and diverfity are in a remarkable degree connected together; but this word has been hitherto thus applied, not fo much from theory, as from mere mechanical fenfation. Any temperament whatever deftroys thefe bands of identity and diverfity, and therefore ought not to be admitted into mufic, unlefs in the way practifed by P. Valloti, and recommended by Tartini.

§ 67.
Trumpet Marine.

Fig. 8.

In order to illuftrate farther the phænomenon reprefented in fig. 6, N° 1, 2, on which all true mufic feems to me to be founded, I will exhibit to the eye what is fuppofed to happen when any homogeneous ftring is founded. It is, as I obferved § 2, a fact agreed on univerfally, that every fuch ftring has an accompaniment of 12th and 17th; i. e. $\frac{1}{3}$ and $\frac{1}{5}$ part of the ftring vibrates, as well as the whole. Let A B, fig. 8, reprefent a mufical ftring; $AD = DE = EB = \frac{1}{3} AB$; $AK = KM = MO = OQ = QB = \frac{1}{5} AB$; $DM = OE = \frac{1}{3} KM = \frac{1}{15} AB$. The ftring A B being founded, will give the note belonging to its totality, and therefore will vibrate in the manner reprefented by the curve A C B; but it will likewife give the 12th, which belongs to each 3d part of the ftring; therefore each third part will vibrate in the manner reprefented by the curves A F D, D G E, E H B: But it will likewife give the 17th, which belongs to each 5th part of the

the string; therefore each 5th of the string will also vibrate in the manner represented by the curves A I K, K L M, M N O, O P Q, Q R B; therefore the points K, D, M, O, E, Q, are comparatively at rest, and not only those, but every 15th part of the string; for D M is $\frac{1}{15}$ of the whole string, being $\frac{1}{5}$ of $\frac{1}{3}$; and being an aliquot of the other parts, and of the whole, must produce analogous vibrations. Were we to add the vibrations of $\frac{1}{7}$ and $\frac{1}{9}$, and combine them with these, the phænomenon would be still more complicated; and yet all these small vibrations certainly exist, and are so far from causing any confusion, that they give the greatest perfection to music.

I own the last-mentioned phænomenon is incomprehensible, and so is every hypothesis that has been invented to explain how the air can possibly convey distinct sounds to the ear in a full concert. Thus all our speculations lead us at last out of our depth: We are obliged frequently to deal with quantities, and other matters of an indefinite nature; in these cases it is our aim, as it is our interest, to circumscribe and bring every object that concerns our pursuits within limits. This aim has produced every system, and every hypothesis, that has disgraced human science. It is not wonderful, however, that so many ingenious men have been tempted into this ocean; where few, very few, escape shipwreck; when we reflect, that knowledge, without a system, consists of nothing but detached scraps, with which the memory is overburthened, and the mind very little enlightened. Lucky is he who happens to circumscribe any portion, however inconsiderable, from the chaos of materials set before us by the Deity, for the employment of our faculties, and, by reducing it to order, renders it fit for our purposes! How far I have succeeded in such an attempt, the world must judge; and, if the general voice is against me, I will say with Huygens, Cosm. p. 10, " If any one shall think that I

" have

Ch. IV.

§ 68. *Difficulty of finding cause.*

Chap. IV. "have spent my time to little or no purpose, in proposing con-
"jectures about things, which we must allow cannot with cer-
"tainty be comprehended: I will answer, that the whole study
"of physics, so far as it is concerned in finding the causes of
"things, must for the same reason be condemned; where the
"highest merit is to find out what is probable; and where the
"investigation either of very important or very obscure truths
"gives delight."

§ 69. But to return to my main business. Tartini next comes to the
Counterpoint. Counterpoint, the essential part of music. He observes, that the 3d, 5th, and 8th, are never marked upon the base where they belong, because in a figured base they are all supposed without marking, where there are no figures at all, as being inseparable from the fundamental base, in consequence of the phænomenon mentioned more than once in this treatise. He then distinguishes the three cadences; viz. that from G above to C below, which he calls the harmonic, because it goes from the harmonic mean to its extreme; from F to C, which he calls the arithmetical, because it goes from the arithmetical mean to its extreme; and the next, from F to G, which he calls the mixt, because it goes from the arithmetical to the harmonic mean. From hence he forms the base notes belonging to the octave, in a way that admits of no dispute. From this base arises modulation, or transition from one harmony to another. Why he has confined the tone of C to this modulation, will be shewn afterwards.

§ 70. He then proceeds to shew, that the common way of figuring
Figuring the the notes of the octave is erroneous; v. g. when a 6th alone is put
octave. to D and A, of which Rameau is guilty as to D, calling it a 4th fundamental. This must be an abuse both of words and harmony; for a fundamental base, in its very idea, supposes no accompaniment

niment but 3d, 5th, and 8th, either direct or reverfed: So much for the words. As to harmony, D never can have the 6th belonging to it, unlefs as 5th of G; in which cafe G is firft fundamental, and not B, or the 6th; and therefore the 4th alfo fhould have been added. This is explained, in the cleareft way, by our author, though it has puzzled the profeffors, who have hitherto had no certain rule to guide them.

CHAP. IV.

Tartini very properly calls C, E, G, which notes are heard in every founding ftring, 1ft, 2d, and 3d bafe, becaufe they are and may be ufed as fuch, only putting the proper figures over, or, as it is called, reverfing the chord, i. e. putting that above which ought to be below: And this idea gives an opportunity of fhewing how all the notes in the octave, if ufed as bafes, ought to be figured; which is very different from the common method, p. 106; but I fhall not enter into the detail, as I could not well explain myfelf without more plates, which fo flight a work does not deferve. However, I thought it right not to pafs over in filence a point of fuch confequence; vide p. 106, 107.

§ 71.
1ft, 2d, and 3d bafes.

He now enters upon a very curious fubject, on which he throws great light; and has put an end to the many difputes that have arifen. The fubject is, the modes of the excellent compofers of the 15th century, who ufed a fcale for prime bafes, which he examines: " This fcale, as being formed of a mixture of the har-
" monical and arithmetical progreffion, has," he fays, " many
" and particular beauties belonging to it; but infeparable from
" a certain crudity of modulation, which many of thofe compofers
" either could not or would not guard themfelves againft." He then fhews, that the crudity or harfhnefs of this fcale proceeds from the tritones neceffarily refulting from it; and propofes a method to avoid this crudity, by making D and A, in the fcale of the oc-

§ 72.
Ancient modes.

tave,

CHAP. IV. tave, fundamental bases, with a third minor; so that every note has 3d, 5th, and 8th for its accompaniment. I shall not particularly mention how he proves the connection between these 3ds minor with the common diatonic; because I think what he says is rather too subtile; but as this connection gives the two fundamental closes in the octave, in a regular manner, there is no reason to doubt but that he is in the right.

§ 73.
Mixt scale.

"The effect of the harmony of this scale," says he, "cannot
"fail of being highly agreeable in its modulations; because it
"includes in itself the two harmonics of 3d major and minor,
"different in that respect from the scale deduced from the harmony
"of the three cadences, (he means those of C, F, and G) which
"consists, by its very nature, of the harmony of the 3d major
"only; and therefore this last, as being wholly of the harmonic
"genus, will have indeed more force; but the other, which has
"a mixture of the harmonic and arithmetical kinds, will have
"more variety and sweetness. Whoever knows how to avail
"himself of one and the other, or of their conjunction, in a
"proper manner, according to the nature of the subject, will
"be able to produce all the effect he aims at."

§ 74.
Discords.

What follows, about resolving discords, I have already considered, in another place; and I find nothing in this chapter that inclines me to alter my opinion.

§ 75.
Measure.

His deduction of the measure from the cadences is curious and new. Common time, as we call it, or measure, arises from the octave, which is as 1 : 2; triple time arises from the 5th, which is as 2 : 3. "These," adds he, "are the utmost limits
"where we can hope to find any thing worth notice. This is
"so true, that many having attempted to introduce other kinds
"of

" of meafure, inftead of a good effect, have found the greateft CHAP. IV.
" confufion; and fo it will always happen." I have feen mufic
with 5 equal notes; but I never faw any body who could perform it.

Our author proceeds to obferve, that the cadences belonging § 76.
to the octave do not arife from the arbitrary rules of arts, but are *Cadences*.
required by nature. " I do not, however," fays he, " draw this
" confequence, that thefe primary examples ought to be an uni-
" verfal unalterable law; if fo, mufic would want the beauty
" arifing from variety: But I will fay, that variety itfelf ought
" to have a pattern to go by, that it may not become extrava-
" gant; and that to determine the cadence where it ought to be,
" and to reduce the fenfe of the mufic, or, in other words, its
" meaning, to a proper period, contributes greatly towards
" unfolding the fubject propofed, and making it clear and in-
" telligible to the hearers."

When words are fet to mufic, the length and fhortnefs of § 77.
fyllables ought to be regarded; in fuch a manner, that a long *Metre*.
fyllable ought to have a longer note belonging to it than a fhorter;
but not only that; for this diftinction may be exactly obferved,
and yet the effect may be very bad, and abfurd; for it is neceffary that the accented part, which is the long fyllable, fhould alfo
be accompanied by the accented part of the mufic. Now, the
accented part of the bar is where the harmony of the key is, which,
in common time, is, or ought to be, in the beginning or middle
of the bar. This Tartini demonftrates in the cleareft manner.
" It is one thing," adds he, " not to chufe to have a cadence
" upon the harmony propofed, for two or three bars, dwelling
" on the fame fundamental bafe; and another thing, whether
" there is not, in fact, a cadence virtually in the greateft part
" of

Chap. IV. " of practical cases; and, in general, whether it is not required
" by nature, in conformity to the primary exemplar in the places
" above mentioned, i. e. the beginning and middle of the bar.
" I am sensible, that prejudice may have some effect, in making
" a whole orchestra accent stronger at these places, especially in
" certain kinds of music, from being used to see it done by their
" director; but this does not hinder me from holding the same
" opinion. The fact is, that, independently of musical habit,
" I have often observed popular and country dances directed by
" a cymbal, an instrument void of any musical sound. Three
" things I have observed upon this occasion; greater and less
" strokes equivalent to long and short; the most exact confor-
" mity with the two kind of measures, common and triple; and
" always stronger strokes in the beginning of each respective
" measure or bar. Being thus convinced by a fact resulting from
" nature, and persuaded, that, in similar circumstances, the
" same thing must happen in every other nation, I am con-
" strained to rely on my theory, supported and proved in such
" a manner as to take away all suspicion of prejudice." The
same thing does actually happen in Persia, by Kœmfer's account.
I shall transcribe what he says about this point, when he is de-
scribing the way of life amongst the inhabitants of Ormuz, during
the hot months, which they pass in the palm-groves, upon the
neighbouring mountains: " The Persian musicians," says he,
Amæn. Exotic. p. 743, " know no rules; they have no skill in
" singing or playing; but they keep well in time, using only
" unisons, or octaves; and vary their rhythm, or time, in so mas-
" terly a manner, that their music not only pleases the ignorant,
" but even the learned; who cannot but wonder, that the com-
" mon people should excel so perfectly in a thing, which we are
" taught with much pains.

Sir Isaac Newton says, Chronol. p. 14, that the Idæi Dactyli "keeping time by striking upon one another's armour with their swords, brought in," i. e. into Greece, "music and poetry." This account seems to me to be highly probable; for rhythmical, or measured motion, always has, in some degree, and always ought to govern, poetry, as well as music. Suppose those country people mentioned by Tartini, who danced to the Cembalo, had prevailed on a poet and a musician to give them words and air to their measures; is it not evident, that one in his closes, and the other in his metre, would have been tied down to the rhythmic motion? Tartini therefore justly lays a great stress upon the rhythm, as the ancients did; for unless this is well marked, music is lifeless, insipid, and, one may say, without a soul, as it is bereaved of that which first produced it. On the contrary, the effect of a well-composed minuet, a jig, or a horn-pipe, on the generality of mankind, is a sufficient proof of the efficacy of rhythm, I may say, of its magic. It is this which gives air to a tune, and which so few musicians have excelled in. Learned and ingenious compositions we have in abundance, such as make a very handsome appearance upon paper; but they are forgotten as soon as the performance is over. I will observe, upon this occasion, that if the blacksmiths hammers ever were of use to music, it must have been by shewing the power and beauty of rhythm; for it behoves all those who work in company at the anvil, to be very careful in keeping time, as great mischief would happen from the want of it.

CHAP. IV

§ 78.

Rhythm.

Nothing is more certain than what was said, in the beginning of § 77, ought to be an inviolable rule in vocal music; viz. that accented syllables ought to be accompanied with accented notes. I will not particularly examine, how far this rule of nature is observed;

§ 79.

Accents musical and metrical.

Chap. IV. ſerved; becauſe, as things go on at preſent, any notes will ſerve for any words: Theſe are ſo frittered away, that they ſeem rather the ghoſts of mangled words, lingering and ſticking to the tongue, like the ghoſts of wicked men, which, as Plato ſays, are frequently ſeen hovering about their tombs. But I will leave them to linger and hover on, according to the mercy of their arbitrary maſters; and return to the dictates of nature, which determine, that muſical and poetical accents ought to go together. This is ſo certain, that no muſician in his ſenſes would, in common time, begin his ſubject, if the verſe is iambic, without putting the ſecond ſyllable at the beginning or middle of the bar, as long as he has any regard to the words at all; whereas, if the verſe is trochaic, he will as certainly put the firſt ſyllable in the aforementioned places.

§ 80.
Iſ. Voſſius
on Rhythm.

Iſaac Voſſius publiſhed a treatiſe concerning vocal muſic and rhythm, in which there are many ingenious and ſolid obſervations, ſhewing how much the antient Greeks ſurpaſſed the moderns, by their attention to the rhythm and metre of their muſic and poetry; that muſic cannot be perfect without this attention; and that the Greek and Roman are more adapted to muſic than any of the modern languages. All theſe propoſitions muſt be allowed to be true; but when he ſays, that, for want of long and ſhort ſyllables, no good muſic can be compoſed at preſent, I think he goes too far. That our proſody is not exact; i. e. that we have not the ſame regard to the quantity of ſyllables, ariſing either from what grammarians call nature, or from poſition, is certain. The Greeks, we know, had fixed rules, by which the quantity of almoſt every ſyllable in their language was determined; and no poet could offend againſt thoſe rules without incurring contempt. The Romans imitated them in this, as in every other art, as far as their genius would allow. But it does by no means follow,

follow, that, becaufe we fall infinitely fhort of the precifion of the antients in this particular, the modern languages will not admit of good vocal mufic. Could Voffius read any modern poetry, and not obferve that it was regulated by accent; now accent implies quantity. It is true, that our fhort fyllables are often loaded with confonants, which makes them very uncouth and difficult to pronounce; and this great defect throws an additional burthen on the finger, which would be avoided in a fmoother language; but fcarcely, if at all, affects the compofer, if the poetical numbers are juft, and the words expreffive. Monfieur Rouffeau has taken up this opinion of Voffius, and applied it to the French language; but, as I do not remember that he has enforced it by any new reafons, I fhall not particularly meddle with this lively writer, and only obferve, that the French language is perhaps lefs capable of being well fet to mufic, than other polite languages in Europe, for many reafons which might be given.

But, whatever the cafe may be with the French language, in relation to mufic, it muft be allowed, that the Italian is not wanting in variety of long and fhort fyllables. They have many words of two fyllables, that are iambic, as così, trovò, virtù, però, &c.; very many that are trochaic, as canto, parla, fono, ufo, &c. which may alfo ferve as fpondees; many words of three fyllables that are dactylic, as trovano, parlano, proffimo, ottimo, &c.; fome anapæfts, as vanità, unità; many that are amphibrachys, or Bacchian, as catena, fidele, alcuno, &c. There is alfo great variety in the words of four fyllables, as curiofo, infinito; intrinfeco, malevŏlo, veriffimo; difficoltà, perpleffità, ebrietà, &c. This variety of accents, joined to the wonderful fmoothnefs of the Italian tongue, gives it a fuperiority, for the purpofe of finging, over all the modern languages, that cannot be difputed. Were it not for this want of fmoothnefs, we might perhaps be

CHAP. IV.

§ 81.
Profody Italian.

English
rivals

CHAP. IV. rivals to the Italians; for some of our words of two syllables are iambic, as detest, employ, belong, &c.; others trochaic, as level, hinder, blessed, kindred, &c.; many of our words of three syllables have the accent on the first, as usury, lenity, villany, &c.; some on the second, as consider, beloved, deliver, &c. The attempt of Sir Philip Sidney, to introduce what is called heroic verse into our language, succeeded so ill in his hands, and has been so much ridiculed ever since, that I was carried away with the stream, and once thought we could not use dactylic feet; but I am convinced of the contrary, and shall now make it evident, to any competent judge, that we not only may, but do use them. Every scholar will own, that the following verse,

Πολλα δ' αναυια καιαυα παραυιατε δογμιατ' ηλθον,

consists of dactylic feet, as being a verse in Homer. Now, add the word γαρ at the beginning of it, and cut it off at παραυ, and I desire to know what difference there is between that, and this well-known English verse,

My | tīme, ŏ yĕ | Mūsĕs, wăs | hăppĭlў | spēnt:

That the metre is fundamentally and essentially the same, is evident from hence, that if any composer was to set these lines to music, he must necessarily accent both on the second syllable; and, which is more to the purpose, the second syllable, and the two following ones, must make a whole bar, or half a one, which is the same thing; and the two last notes of the bar together should in strictness be equal only to the first by itself. N. B. The redundant syllable, *spent*, at the end of this verse, joined to the first syllable of the next, and so on, keeps up the rhythm throughout the whole song.

§ 82.
Discordant notes.

I wish it were consistent with my design, to give a full account of Tartini's doctrine on this head, which is very clear, and very instructive to musicians; but, besides that many plates would be required,

required, I always meant to refer the inquisitive reader to the original. After having given an example of the right manner of using discordant notes, with reference to cadences, he says, "In-finite deductions arise from this example, as a first principle, which may be equivalent to an entire practical treatise. But my intention is to establish first principles, exemplified so far as is necessary, and no more." He then adds the following musical canon: "*You may confine the discordant notes within li-mits, as much less as you please than half the bar; but never ought to let them exceed it.* There may," says he, "be some excep-tions, in regard to such modes of musical expression as are fa-miliar to the reigning taste, in which no scruple is made to substitute the shadow for the substance; i. e. instead of the fundamental notes of the song, to give us those which are de-duced from them. According to this taste, the discordant notes may very well be placed in the beginning and middle of the bar; but this, being a more than ordinary poetical licence of the present age, does not affect the truth of the above-men-tioned canon."

Chap. IV.

Tartini enters next upon a most perplexed and intricate subject, viz. the chromatic and enharmonic systems of the Greeks; which though he does not pretend to have cleared up, yet he has evi-dently shewn, that either these genera have been totally misun-derstood by the moderns; or that the antients used them in direct opposition to the first principles of harmony. He has given an example of his own, in the chromatic, which is practicable, and which proceeds by two hemitones following one another, and an uncompounded interval consisting of three hemitones. Now this is perfectly conformable to what all the Greek writers on music call the chromatic; but this in reality seems to be nothing more than a common passage from a 3d major to a 3d minor. It may

§ 83.
Antient chro-matic.

[56]

CHAP. IV. be asked then, How this chromatic happens to be practicable, and the antient not? The answer is, That the antients began theirs, as is generally thought, from a note that was distant from the next above it by a hemitone; v. g. from B to C, and from thence to C✱, and E, which completed the tetrachord, but which led into a tone which had no relation to the first: Whereas Tartini sets out from G, then goes to G✱, A, and C. This method carries him from C 3d major to A 3d minor; which two keys are most intimately connected. I shall have an opportunity of giving an idea of another chromatic, by the assistance of Tartini, but not according to the antient system; which is, I believe, as well as many other things relating to the Greek music, a perfect enigma; though we have so many considerable old writers on that subject, and so many commentators upon them; some proofs of this I shall offer in the course of the present work. A plain proof that the antient and modern chromatic are intirely different, is, that, according to Aristoxenus, two tones cannot follow one another in that genus; p. 65.

§ 84.
Antient enharmonic.

Tartini, after having examined the supposed chromatic of the antients, proceeds to the enharmonic, which he likewise finds to be contrary to the principles of harmony: But he undertakes to give one of his own, by means of a note, as he says, out of the limits of the hexachord, expressed by $\frac{1}{7}$, which he calls a consonance; giving us to understand that is a note arising from nature, and is founded with the greatest facility on the trumpet marine and German horn. But when he comes to give an example of the use of this note along with the base, it appears not to be the note he imagined. B♭, it is true, which is expressed by $\frac{1}{7}$, when C is principal note, stands against C in the base, and very properly; but C here is 5th of the tone; for the tone is F; and therefore B♭, as he marks it, is not 7th, as it ought to be, but 4th, of F. The whole is cleared up, when he transposes his example

ample out of F into C; for then G with the 7th minor is nothing but the common chord, in passing from the 5th of the tone to the close, and therefore requires no particular resolution, as appears both by common practice and by theory; for F 7th of G is a confonant note, that joins the harmonic and arithmetic fyftem together. It is true, he lowers F natural; but owns afterwards, that it is fo near the truth, that it does not in the leaft deftroy the fine effect of the harmony.

From what has been faid, it appears that our author has not difcovered the enharmonic, any more than others, who have attempted it before; but he has however kept within the bounds of harmony, with that fobriety and excellent tafte, which never fuffer him to go wrong in practice, however he may fometimes be mifled by his theory. But Monfieur Rameau, Generat. Harmon. p. 153, not altogether fo well qualified in thofe refpects, undertook to give us an enharmonic fyftem, not only in theory but in practife; for he fays he had introduced it into one of his operas. He owns honeftly indeed, that it had not all the effect he expected from it; but this he attributes, as is ufual in fuch cafes, to the bad execution of the performers. He had more reafon, in my opinion, to take all the blame to himfelf; for his enharmonic confifts in one of the groffeft paralogifms that ever entered into the head of a mufician. It is a thing well known, that on the harpfichord the fame key is made ufe of for two different notes, belonging to harmonies, that have no relation to one another. What then is the art of Monfieur Rameau? Why truly, nothing more nor lefs than, by help of this ambiguous way of marking two notes, to join two harmonies together that ought never to meet. This method he dignifies with the name of enharmonic; and fays, that it makes you feem to pafs in an inftant from one hemifphere to another; an excellent conceit this, no doubt, to recommend mufic,

CHAP. IV.

§ 85. *Enharmonic of Monfieur Rameau.*

I   which

Chap. IV. which, from the earliest times down to our own, has furnished all the civilised part of the world with ideas of beauty arising from identity and diversity combined together. But if he had a fancy to hurry his audience to the antipodes in so precipitate a manner, why not begin with A natural, 3d major; and, after having well settled the tone, step at once boldly into E♭, 3d major; which would have answered his purpose full as well. But to return to Tartini.

§ 86.
Tritones.

He observes, that in going through the octave with the full accompaniment, the inconcinnous interval of a Tritone between F and B arises; which he says has a very good effect in ascending, as the progress is from worse to better, i. e. from the arithmetic to the harmonic system; but that in descending it is by no means to be allowed, and is an error when practised. I should rather think, that the reason of this difference is, that in ascending F, which makes a tritone with B in the next chord, becomes afterwards the 7th of G, and so is resolved, as belonging properly to it, before the close in C: whereas in descending to the next chord, which is C E G, F cannot be held on, and consequently there can be no resolution. It appears to me evident, that there is no possibility of going through the octave in counterpoint without a discord, and therefore the octave, considered as proceeding by tones and hemitones, is merely artificial. Tartini's last observation is a proof of this; for if every note were natural throughout the scale, i. e. if the succession were natural, it would be quite indifferent whether we ascend or descend, as in the diatonic hexachord and heptachord.

§ 87.
Perfection of the diatonic.

I am now coming to the conclusion of the 4th chapter, and shall give some of his observations on the doctrines contained in it, in his own words, as follows. " In relation to the universal
" dissonant

" diſſonant ſyſtem, the fundamental harmony by which the dif- CHAP. IV.
" ſonances are regulated is always diatonic; as there is not,
" nor can be, any caſe, in which a diſſonance is founded on any
" other notes but the 3d, 5th, and 8th. Here then is explained
" by practiſe what I undertook to prove demonſtratively in the
" ſecond chapter, in relation to the hexachord, as to the period
" and completion of the phyſico-harmonic ſyſtem, in its utmoſt
" extent." I omit ſome lines, which would be unintelligible to
thoſe who have not read the original; after which, he goes on
thus: " We find, that the diatonic ſyſtem is regulated by itſelf,
" and is compleat by itſelf; and therefore it was uſed by the
" Greeks, by the old Italian compoſers, and is uſed by us at
" preſent, whenever we pleaſe, according to the rigor of its na-
" ture and conſtitution. We find laſtly, that whatever addition
" is made to it, may be a regular conſequence, but can never
" be neceſſary; for whatever is more than the diatonic, although
" it is a different mode of harmony, is not a different ſubſtance.
" As a ſubſtance, it is deduced from the hexachord; and it is
" impoſſible to alter it either in theory or practiſe." In this I
perfectly agree with my maſter; and it is not without much regret
that I have been forced ſo frequently to diſſent from him, in this
as well as the foregoing chapters. I can only ſay, by way of
apology, that I was very far from ſetting out with an intent to
criticiſe. I had, and ſtill have, the higheſt opinion of his performance; but the light which he himſelf afforded enabled me
to diſcover another path, that ſeemed to me more ſure and leſs
intricate. Had I not been led into it by his aſſiſtance, in all probability I had never made the uſe I have done of the trumpet
marine; though I had long ſurmiſed, that it might, in ſome way
or other, be turned to better purpoſes than what it had been applied to. It has already, I hope, been not unſucceſsfully employed; but its uſe will ſtill be more evident before I have done,

ſhould

CHAP. IV. should I not happen to be misled by that overweening fondness which all men have for their own productions, and which therefore stands in need of no apology. Fere unumquemq; sua sibi velle cogitata parere, et parta fovere, nec novum est, nec usque adeo intolerandum. Valsalva.

§ 88.
A summary view of the next chapter.

I have now gone through four chapters out of six, which make the whole of my author's treatise. If I have done tolerable justice to this excellent work, I have no doubt but that all my musical readers, I mean of the profession, will have a great curiosity to consult the original; others perhaps, not unskilled in music, may be contented barely to see what principles their art is founded upon. This is a curiosity which I can hardly suppose any lover of music to be without: But, however that may be, I am now coming to a part of the work, which must interest every one who pretends to taste in this way; because it contains the judgment of the greatest of all modern masters, on a subject that very much divides the musical world. As this part of my work will be much more entertaining to some of my readers, so it will be much easier for me to execute. Instead of picking out what I looked upon as essential, in order to give some idea of the new principles with which the original abounds; instead of taking pains to reduce these principles into the narrowest compass possible, and putting them in the clearest light I was able; lastly, instead of taking no small pains to understand my author's doctrines, which are sometimes very obscure, I shall not have much to do, in the following chapter, but to translate.

CHAP. V.
§ 89.
Introduction.

Tartini begins his 5th chapter in the following manner: " As, " from the difference of musical keys, and from the different po- " sition of the common diatonic scale, the modes or musical tones, " which are an essential part of our church-music, and still more
" so

" so of the antient Greek music, are deduced, this chapter be- CHAP. V.
" comes neceſſary; in which, however, there is hardly any thing
" demonſtrative, and very little phyſical. Hitherto I have ſailed
" through an ocean of my own, and have always been ſure of
" my courſe; but to obey you, illuſtrious Sir," addreſſing him-
" ſelf to his friend, " I muſt now enter into another ocean, unex-
" plored hitherto by any one, and do not know what will be my
" fate. Do not therefore expect from me, in this chapter, that
" boldneſs, which ariſes from a conſciouſneſs of truth; ſuch as
" you have ſeen in the preceding chapters. Look favorably,
" however, on this real ſacrifice of my obedience, as I enter on
" ſo nice a ſubject without any ſure guide; knowing how deſirous
" you are to go to the bottom of a matter ſo truly intereſting."

" The ſubſtance of what I am going to undertake, is, on one § 90.
" ſide, the diſcovery of the muſical modes; by the means of *Muſical modes*
" which, and of poetry, the antient Greeks excited and appeaſed, *of the Greeks.*
" at their pleaſure, the paſſions of the human mind: And, on the
" other ſide, the compariſon of the antient modes with our mo-
" dern modes. In order to reduce to the greateſt clearneſs poſ-
" ſible, an affair the moſt involved and obſcure that can employ
" one's thoughts, it is neceſſary, in the firſt place, to underſtand
" what is meant by the word mode. A mode then, in general,
" according to the antient meaning, (called by the Greeks by the
" name of trope, harmony, &c.) ſignifies a ſong determined by
" rule, as to gravity and acuteneſs; as to intervals; as to aſcent
" and deſcent; as to muſical accents, relative to the metre; and
" as to the inſtrument which accompanied the ſong of the muſical
" poet. Thus again, as the matter, treated by the poet, was
" melancholy, or chearful; decent, or laſcivious; furious and
" bacchanalian, or grave and religious; &c. ſo there were de-
" termined and ſpecific modes with the particular conditions of

" certain

CHAP. V. "certain limits as to gravity and acuteneſs; of certain accents
"relative to a certain metre, and a certain inſtrument. Every
"mode had its particular name, as Dorian, Phrygian, Lydian,
"Æolian, &c. and was adapted preciſely to that particular mat-
"ter for which it was inſtituted."

§ 91.
Accounts of them vary.

"The above-mentioned account of the antient modes is all we
"can gather with certainty and clearneſs from hiſtory; and in this
"all hiſtorians antient and modern agree, ſome more, ſome leſs.
"If, in vertu of this account, it is expected that we ſhall be able
"to point out the individual above-mentioned circumſtances, the
"caſe is deſperate; becauſe the antient hiſtories, and much more
"the modern, contradict one another; and what is ſtill worſe,
"monuments and examples are entirely wanting. It ſeems there-
"fore a natural conſequence, that one may reaſonably doubt
"whether the account is true or not; but, in ſpite of doubts
"about the truth of the accounts found in antient hiſtorians,
"concerning the Greek muſic, ſuch are the antients who give
"thoſe accounts, that it would be the height of raſhneſs not to
"believe them. Plato and Ariſtotle are all who need be named
"on this occaſion, and ought to make us bow down our heads.
"Should you aſk me, if ſuch a dominion over the paſſion is poſ-
"ſible in nature? I anſwer frankly, Yes; becauſe I am a wit-
"neſs myſelf of the poſſibility of it, from many inſtances; one

Remarkable effect of muſic.

"of which I will relate. In the year 1714, (if I am not miſtaken)
"in an opera that was performed at Ancona, there was, in the
"beginning of the third act, a paſſage of recitative, unaccom-
"panied by any other inſtrument but the baſe; which raiſed,
"both in the profeſſors and in the reſt of the audience, ſuch and
"ſo great a commotion of mind, that we could not help ſtaring
"at one another, on account of the viſible change of color
"that was cauſed in every one's countenance. The effect was

"not

" not of the plaintive kind: I remember well, that the words
" expressed indignation; but of so harsh and chilling a nature,
" that the mind was disordered by it. Thirteen times this drama
" was performed, and the same effect always followed, and that
" too universally; of which the remarkable previous silence of
" the audience, to prepare themselves for the enjoyment of the
" effect, was an undoubted sign.

" I was too young to think of preserving a copy of this pas- § 92.
" sage, and have since been very sorry I did not. That the *Want of prin-*
" composer, though excellent in his time, knew by principle that *ciples among*
" such an effect would be produced, I do not believe; but I be- *the moderns.*
" lieve, that, being a man of very fine taste, and great judgment,
" he was led by good sense, and by the words, and had, on that
" occasion, accidentally hit upon the truth of nature. From
" hence I conclude, that if we know how to give a beginning to
" commotion, on the other hand, we have not principles to guide
" us in the progress. The fact is, that in small movements, and
" for a little time, a lucky hit of this sort oftentimes happens
" amongst composers; but there is no rule nor science to attain
" this end in many movements, and for a considerable time.
" This is all that I can advance with certainty upon the subject
" before us, and the possibility of the facts reported, in relation
" to the antient modes of music.

" As to our modern modes, which are also called tones, al- § 93.
" though we know their nature with certainty, yet it is not so *Modern modes.*
" clear what their number is. Common practise, and ecclesi-
" astical custom, have established eight; Zarlino pretends that
" there are twelve; others are of another opinion. But their
" number is of no consequence for the present purpose; it is
" sufficient that we know their formation and nature. These
" consist

CHAP. V. "confift intrinfically in the common diatonic fcale, confidered
"in the full extent of the octave, in its harmonic and arithmetic
"divifion, and in the diverfity as to the place of the hemitones
"in the fcale; which diverfity does not, nor can, proceed from
"any other principle, but that of beginning the fcale with dif-
"ferent notes."

§ 94.
Old Italian modes.

Tartini proceeds to fhew the eight modes ufed by the old Italian mafters; four of which arife from the harmonic divifion of the octave, and are what they called authentic; the other four are what they called plagal, and arife from the arithmetical divifion of the octave. "There were certain rules and laws," fays he, "for the fong, and the refpective clofes; fo that, from the fing-"ing part and the cadence, every tone is known. This is the "fubftance of our modes, or tones. Neverthelefs, I have found "the adjective Dorian annexed to the firft tone, with thefe words, "*adapted to the grave affections*; Hypodorian to the fecond, "*adapted to infpire cheerfulnefs*; Phrygian to the third, *adapted* "*to excite anger*; Hypophrygian to the fourth, *adapted to bring* "*on tranquillity*; &c. You will eafily believe that I am not per-"fwaded of thefe effects; on the contrary, I am perfwaded that "thefe modes have no connection with thofe of the antients; "and I am moreover perfwaded, that their inftitution is not per-"fectly right."

§ 95.
Number of modes.

Our author then proceeds to prove this laft allegation in the cleareft manner; and fhews, that the number is really eight, and no more; but not the fame which the old Italians made ufe of. Both C and A may be either authentic or plagal, i. e. with an harmonic or arithmetical mean. D and F can only be authentic; laftly, E and G can only be plagal. Thus has Tartini cleared up, in a fhort manner, that which has ever been a matter of de-
bate

bate amongst musicians, who had no principles to guide CHAP. V.
them.

 " But this," says he, " only by the bye. I now return to my § 96.
" first point; which is, to say the truth, not to discover, but *Antient and*
" rather to give my conjectures about, the antient modes; to *modern modes compared.*
" explain the modern modes; and to compare them together.
" But the antient ones are in a higher degree more difficult to
" explain, than the moderns are easy; and therefore their com-
" pleat comparison is impossible; for which reason, this chapter
" ought to end here. However, as in obedience to your com-
" mands I am obliged to proceed, whatever I shall add, shall be
" faithfully distinguished into proper classes, of certainty, doubt,
" and opinion.

 " To begin with what is certain. The first thing then is, what § 97.
" I said before, that the antient modes were totally different *Music should*
" from ours. I do not take any merit to myself in proving this, *be subservient to prosody.*
" because this has been proved over and over again; however,
" the method I shall take will be different, and will serve to lead
" me to something of importance. First then, the intervals of
" the antient modes are totally different from ours: Aristides
" enumerates six of these modes; (it is not worth while to give
" them, at length, with their names;) in all which there ought to
" be the enharmonic diesis; whereas our modes, being founded
" on the diatonic or common scale, neither have, nor can have,
" such an interval; which is entirely unknown amongst us, and
" which we cannot execute. The antient modes were so rigorously
" joined to the prosody, that the people could discover the mis-
" takes, if there were any, committed by the musical poet, in
" the length and shortness of the syllables, both in relation to the
" poetry and the music. This is a point of history in which all
        K   " writers

CHAP. V. " writers agree; this gives us an idea quite different from what
" our modern modes, and our mufic in general, furnifh : For,
" to fpeak freely, we make the profody fubfervient to the mufic,
" not the mufic to the profody. Nay farther, by the laws pre-
" fcribed to the antient muficians, to preferve rigoroufly in the
" mufic the quantity of fyllables, it was impoffible to protract
" a vowel, in finging, beyond the time which belonged to
" the fyllable : We, on the contrary, prolong the vowels
" through many bars, although they are oftentimes fhort; as in
" amen, adoro, &c."

§ 98.
The fame fub-
ject continued.

I cannot help expreffing, on this occafion, my perfect agreement with Tartini, that nothing feems more contrary to order,
than the method, mentioned by him, of making the profody fubfervient to the mufic. It feems to me impoffible to produce the
proper effect of vocal mufic this way; and muficians, who have
any regard to their reputation, ought never to indulge the vanity
of a poet, who will, without running any rifk to his own character, undertake fuch a tafk. However, if it fhould ever be
neceffary, for particular reafons, to fet words to mufic, the poet
ought never to make ufe of rhyme; which, by the bye, is fo
much labor loft, in all mufical dramas; for who ever reads the
poetry without the mufic, except the author ? When free from
thefe fhackles, the poet has certainly a much better chance of
fucceeding, at leaft in a tolerable degree; but then he ought to
be very exact in the metre.

§ 99.
Profody rigo-
roufly obferv-
ed.

" You will afk me," continues Tartini, " If it is really pof-
" fible to preferve rigoroufly, in mufic, the quantity of fyllables?
" I anfwer, That it is poffible, not only in the genus, but in the
" fpecies and individual alfo; becaufe, as was faid before, in
" the value of mufical notes there is every thing neceffary for
" the

"the purpose. Nevertheless, we must distinguish, Either the value of the syllable is taken with the utmost rigor, or with a latitude: If with rigor, it is past all doubt, that one long syllable is equal in value to two short ones, just as a minim is equal to two half-minims; and one of these is equal to a crotchet, &c." Tartini then subjoins an instance of the rigorous method, in a verse of Virgil, set to notes, both in common and triple time.

"With these examples," says he, "I mean nothing more, than to shew what progress of musical notes results in each of these times, when they are reduced rigorously to the value of the syllables: But I do not pretend, that the syllables, disposed in such a manner by the measure or bar, should correspond exactly to the sense of the music; as would follow, from what was said in the preceding chapter, relating to the long and short accents of the measure. Whether this was the practise of the Greeks, is more than I know; but something like it must have been the case, by absolute necessity, if it was necessary that the long syllables should be distinguished from the short, in their music. But my opinion is, that the measure amongst the Greeks was observed, not rigorously, but with discretion. If they were real imitators of nature; and if, by the means of poetry joined to music, they raised and calmed the passions; they must of necessity have attended to what happens in common discourse. When this is animated by passion, the natural effect is, in proportion to the passion, a greater or less inflexion of the voice; a greater or less pitch and force of tone; a greater or less lengthening of words and syllables, &c. In the expression a word of more significance occurs: This, without any reflexion, is placed in a stronger point of light than others, by hurrying

§ 100.
Observed with discretion.

"over

CHAP. V. "over it, if the paffion is anger; by dwelling upon it, if the
"paffion is grief; &c.

§ 101.
How the paf-
fions are to be
imitated.

"The mufical poet, if he was alfo a philofopher, being obliged
"to conform to nature, muft have met with many cafes, where
"the long fyllable ought to be lengthened, the fhort fyllables fhor-
"tened, without regard to their rigorous natural value, in order to
"exprefs the paffions properly; and that in comparifon with the
"natural value of other fyllables, which were not fubfervient to the
"paffion, unlefs in preparing the mind for it. A difcretionary,
"therefore, and not a rigorous, regard to bars was neceffary: If
"fo, their mufic refembled the recitative of our Italian operas, in
"which the bars are difcretionary; nay, it can hardly be perceived
"that there are any bars at all. Thus it ought to be, if we under-
"take to imitate the nature of any paffion; which, however con-
"ftant it may be, will not admit of having its motions, which by
"their nature are unequal, regulated by equality. No feries there-
"fore of equal bars can correfpond to fuch an idea; nay, the
"change of time from common to triple, or the contrary, cannot
"correfpond to it; becaufe in all the variations of time, there is ftill
"the equality of movements that conftitute the time. In fimple
"narration there may be an equality of movements, and confe-
"quently, there may be regular bars rigoroufly obferved. If it
"is true, as I think it is, that in order to affect others, we muft
"ourfelves be affected, there are very few narrative parts, which,
"if we follow nature, will admit of being regulated by an equal
"movement; becaufe there are few fuch parts totally free from
"paffion."

§ 102.
Difcretionary
meafure.

"I am confirmed in my opinion, by obferving that difcretionary
"meafure not only can never be of prejudice to the value of fyl-
"lables,

"lables, but, on the contrary, helps infinitely to determine their "quality, if we attend to one rule only; which is, to give in "every cafe at leaft a double quantity of time to a long fyllable, "in proportion to what is given to the fhort one. Who can "doubt, if to the word Barbara a minim and two cretchets are "fet, whereby the dactyl is rigoroufly expreffed as to time; and "to the fame word a minim and two quavers are fet, which is "the difcretionary time; but that the firft fyllable is long; the "like may be faid of the two fhort fyllables? On the contrary, "we fhall be more certain of the value of the fyllables in the fe- "cond way than in the firft. Hence arifes an infinite advantage "to the mufical poet, for imitating nature with the greateft eafe. "And if we, having the fame end in view, fhould follow this "method, why will we imagine the Greeks did otherwife? "Hitherto, I think, I have not deviated from what I pro- "pofed; which was to compare the antient modes with the "modern; becaufe, the comparifon being abfolutely necef- "fary, in order to difcover what kind of mufic it was that "conftituted the antient modes, what I have faid, and what "I fhall fay, of a like kind, muft belong to my fubject. This "notice becomes abfolutely neceffary, becaufe, in purfuing the "comparifon, I fhall give myfelf up to be guided by nature "and reafon, till I come to comprehend what both one and the "other means. I fhall adhere clofely to my argument in the "fubftance, perhaps not in the order. But to proceed.

CHAP. V.

"To our modern modes is joined fimultaneous harmony, "formed by the union of different voices, bafe, tenor, contralto, "and foprano. You know I am no fcholar; neverthelefs, by "good luck, I am not unacquainted with the famous difpute, "whether the antients knew and practifed harmony in our fenfe "of the word. In this queftion, we muft neceffarily recur to the

§ 103. *Simultaneous notes.*

"common

CHAP. V. " common fountain, which is nature. The human species is the
" same, the passions are the same. In this case, their different
" modifications, relating to times, customs, laws, education,
" government, &c. being of no importance, and it sufficing for
" our present purpose, that the foundation is the same, I think
" I shall not be mistaken, if, upon this sure foundation, which
" the Greeks had in common with us, I advance the following
" proposition; That, if simultaneous harmony was known to the
" Greeks, they could not, and ought not to use it, in order to
" arrive at the end they proposed; but ought to employ a single
" voice in their songs.

§ 104.
Effect of simultaneous notes.

" If the intent of the Greeks was to excite, not any general af-
" fection, but a particular and specific passion; it is as certain
" as that nature cannot err, that every passion has its particular
" movements, and its particular tone of voice. I will take for
" an example the most universal and most opposite passions, joy
" and grief: Joy has its sprightly movement, and its intense and
" acute tone of voice: Grief has its slow movement, and its
" low and languid tone; and this in general. In proportion to
" the greater or less degree of each respective passion (as long as
" it remains within its limits and in its nature) both movement
" and voice alter likewise. This is the course of nature; and
" every one of us knows, from his own experience, that what I
" say is true, if he does but reflect. Now, I ask, How is it pos-
" sible, according to nature, that the harmony of four voices,
" the extremes of which are the base, and the soprano, should
" succeed in exciting. properly to mirth, when there is an in-
" trinsic opposition in the conjunction of acute and grave; one
" belonging to mirth, the other to cheerfulness? But it will be
" said, that this defect is supplied by movement, which for that
" purpose may be sprightly in the soprano. This is very well
" for

" for one part, but ill for the whole; becauſe a certain move- CHAP. V.
" ment and a particular voice belong to every paſſion; not a
" movement ſeparated from the voice, nor a voice ſeparated
" from the movement. This, I believe, is the cauſe of what often
" happens, when we hear a well-compoſed and well-executed
" muſical performance. We cannot deny that we feel in our-
" ſelves a beginning of commotion, in general, of the nature of
" the paſſion intended to be raiſed; but as for the progreſs and
" ſpecific determination of it, I have never known it, becauſe I
" never felt in myſelf the intire effect: My own opinion is, that
" ſuch a progreſs is impoſſible, and ſuch a compleat effect, on
" account of the contraſt above-mentioned between the extreme
" parts of the harmony; becauſe, being extremes, and conſe-
" quently of a general nature, it is impoſſible they can unite to-
" gether, ſo as to produce a particular effect. The effect
" will be general, as is the cauſe. There will therefore be a
" tendency towards a certain paſſion; there will never be a
" paſſion ſpecifically determined.

" I muſt add, to come to particulars, that ſuch a movement § 105.
" and ſuch a voice ought to be joined to a ſong adapted to a *Simultaneous*
" particular paſſion. To confine myſelf to the diatonic ſcale, *notes more*
" *particularly*
" in which the Greeks and the moderns agree, and which is *conſidered.*
" ſufficient for our preſent purpoſe: A proper ſong cannot be
" compoſed but with a certain number, and certain kinds of inter-
" vals; hemitone, tone, the two 3ds greater and leſſer, the 4th,
" the 5th, the two 6ths greater and leſſer, the two 7ths greater
" and leſſer, and the octave. Theſe are all. The reſt is only
" repetition and complication. The intrinſic nature of theſe in-
" tervals, and particularly of the ſimple ones, that make up the
" whole harmony, i. e. the octave, the 5th, the 4th, the two
" 3ds major and minor, is not uniform; it is different; and

" that

CHAP. V. " that in such a degree, that using one interval or another in the
" composition of the song, makes a very sensible difference in
" the effect. Let us suppose then, that in general the interval
" of the 3d major corresponds with mirth; and therefore let a
" song be composed, to the base of which belongs specifically
" the 3d major; let the filling up in general consist of 3ds
" major and minor, and let the marked accent, by vertue of the
" bar, fall on the above-mentioned 3ds; so that they may be-
" come more perceptible; let also the movement of the song
" be quick, and let it be sung by a soprano, that there may be
" all the necessary conditions possible. Such a song will have,
" by supposition, every thing proper to excite mirth. Put it
" now into harmony, and it is certain, that while the part of the
" soprano passes successively through the intervals of 3ds, the
" harmony of the base, tenor, and contralto, will proceed simul-
" taneously and successively through the intervals of octave, 5th,
" 4th, 6th, tone, hemitone, &c. according to the different dis-
" position of the voices that fill up the harmony, and according
" to the different passage of the base from one tone to another.
" Now, how is it possible, that, in such a contrast of so many
" different simultaneous intervals of harmony, which must have
" more force than successive intervals of the upper part, should
" produce the effect for which the song was formed? It is not
" enough, to say, that the soprano, as being in the extreme, and
" consequently more intense and over-ruling, will be heard dis-
" tinctly in comparison of the other voices, and therefore will
" produce its effect. This proposition is false in harmony. Three
" voices against one will prevail, although the single voice be
" more intense, the three more remiss. This is certain in prac-
" tise, when the voices are proportionate. But let us grant the
" proposition: I ask, if, whether in favor of the voices joined
" in order to compleat the harmony, there will or will not be
" a dis-

" a diſtraction in the mind of the hearer, as being forced to CHAP. V.
" liſten both to the principal voice and its aſſociates? It cannot
" be denied, there will certainly be a diſtraction; and this is ſuf-
" ficient to deſtroy the main intent.

" It is not a light taſk to undertake to raiſe, by the means of   § 106.
" poetry and muſic, a determinate paſſion. I, for my own part, *Simultaneous*
" believe it is much more difficult than that which an orator *harmony in-*
conſiſtent with
" undertakes, when he attempts to move and perſuade; nay, *expreſſion.*
" I believe it to be the moſt difficult taſk, that can be undertaken,
" in the whole compaſs of human affairs. To obtain this, it is
" neceſſary for the muſician to bring the human mind to a per-
" fect attention, nay, to an intenſeneſs of attention. It is im-
" poſſible to attain this, as long as there is the leaſt diſtraction;
" this is a truth which I have from nature; it is no production
" of my own brain: It is therefore impoſſible to excite ſuch a
" determinate paſſion, by the means of a ſong joined to harmony,
" in our ſenſe of the word; and at moſt, as I ſaid above, a be-
" ginning of commotion in general is all that is poſſible. If the
" Greeks therefore knew harmony in our ſenſe, they ought not,
" nor could they, avail themſelves of it, for the end they had in
" view; becauſe, in regard to principles of nature, in which all
" men certainly reſemble one another, we ourſelves, who know
" harmony, muſt be conſtrained to exclude it, and make uſe of
" a ſingle voice, if we propoſe to attain the ſame end.

" I have often uſed the expreſſion, *harmony underſtood by*   § 107.
" *the Greeks in our ſenſe of the word.* I will explain myſelf. *Greeks did not*
" It cannot be denied, that the Greeks in ſome ſenſe underſtood *uſe ſimulta-*
neous harmo-
" harmony; becauſe in their hiſtories, their philoſophy, their *ny.*
" monuments, this word continually occurs. But farther; They
" called the octave, the 5th, the 4th, conſonant intervals; and
" all

CHAP. V. "all intervals less than the 4th, dissonances. Their harmony
"therefore was not, like ours, composed of simultaneous, but
"successive notes; and they meant (to speak in our way) that
"the passage to the 4th, 5th, and octave was harmonious, and
"consequently consonant; and that the notes which fill up the
"4th were dissonant. They had therefore formed their tetra-
"chords, or passages to the 4th, as props of consonant har-
"mony; and these, according to the different genera of music,
"viz. diatonic, chromatic, and enharmonic, were filled up with
"different divisions."

§ 108.
Whether such music is best can scarcely be doubted.

I doubt not but that many people will be amazed to find Tartini speak so strongly against simultaneous harmony, and be apt to look on all he has said, or can say, as not worth their notice: But I desire that they will consider this as the opinion of a man perfectly well qualified to judge, both from his situation, and his extraordinary genius for music; and that it is probable, nothing but conviction could induce him to speak in this manner, considering all the prejudices that must naturally lie on the other side of the question, from the prevailing fashion in his own country; where music flourishes more than in any other part of the world, and where genius is more able to cover defects, if they can be covered, by the elegance of the composition and the brilliancy of the execution. His authority, therefore, ought at least to go thus far, viz. to make us suspend our judgment till a fair trial has been made: Nay, I may say, that something like a trial has been made; and, when it has been made by a composer of genius, has always succeeded. Those feelings of nature, which, as Tartini observes, are and must be common to us and the Greeks, have of late years put the Italian masters upon working the parts less in their opera music; and have produced those thrumming bases, as they are called by our harmonists, by way of ridicule.

Operas

Operas succeeded the old church music, where the parts were CHAP. V. worked with great judgment and labor, and where they produced a great effect, as none of the common passions were to be excited, § 109. and only a pomp of solemn and grave harmony was or ought to *Old church-* be expected; for I look upon the *miserere's* and *stabat mater's* of *music.* later masters to be deviations from the genuine old church stile. I can for myself say, that I never was so little pleased with music, as with what I heard in the churches in Italy; it being so ill suited to the solemnity of the place, and the occasion; and some of my friends expressed the same sentiments: So that, as church-music at first carried a bad taste into opera-music, the reverse afterwards took place, and church-music now suffers, in its turn, from the influence of its fashionable rival.

The last-mentioned perversion of music is of more consequence § 110. than the former, and much more blameable. If we are suffered *Corruption of* to enjoy perfect tranquillity at the theatre, while the singer, or *church-music.* at least the composer, means to plunge us into all the tumult of varying passions, the hurt is not great. But in the church, to substitute gay airs, or passionate expression, in the room of solemn music, is a perversion that defeats the great end for which music was first instituted, as appears by the unanimous testimony of history. We know that this was the case amongst the Jews; and it is no less certain, that it was the case amongst the pagans. I shall content myself with producing one single proof of this assertion out of Plutarch; who says thus, Vol. II. p. 1140:
‘ Amongst the Greeks, in antient times, theatrical music was
‘ not so much as known. Music then was wholly employed
‘ for divine worship, the instruction of youth, and the praise
‘ of illustrious heroes; and again, p. 1131, it is a part of
‘ piety, and even a principal duty of man, to sing hymns to
‘ the gods, who have given to man alone an articulate voice.’

I now

Chap. V. I now return to my author, who having shewed, in a way peculiar to himself, that the Greek music turned entirely upon the tetrachords, which he properly calls the props of harmony, proceeds thus: " We have many examples in the
§ 111.
Old Italian music.
" old church-music, which is all of the diatonic kind, of
" cadences formed by the hemitone major descending. I
" should be apt to think, that, amongst the antient songs, there
" are some genuine ones according to the example of the Greeks,
" if it was not for the entire contrast between the music and the
" prosody. It must be owned, that there are some so full of gra-
" vity, majesty, and sweetness, joined to the most perfect mu-
" sical simplicity, that we moderns should find it a very hard
" task to rival them. An inquiry into their date is of little im-
" portance; their musical nature is all we want. It is certain
" then, that they were made for a single voice; if this voice was
" multiplied by the unisons of a whole people, that does not de-
" rogate from the design of the institution; because unison is in
" its ratio only one voice; that they are simple in the highest
" degree; that they partake of the nature of recitative, but largo;
" that many of them are like canzoni, or songs, many of a mixt
" nature; that none are confined to regular bars, but discretionary;
" and that in each of them the key is determined, and is limited
" by a convenient extent, as to grave and acute." This idea is in general conformable to nature; and, with regard to the universality of circumstances, it is impossible to contrive with more simplicity; nor could the Greeks themselves have contrived or intended otherwise.

§ 112.
Idea of the Greek music.
" The Greeks being, with respect to us, the first institutors
" of music, it follows, that they set out with this idea of sim-
" plicity; because, however capable men may be of using art
" and refinement, yet, in the first invention and institution
" of

"of things, it is certain, that nature does all, art nothing; CHAP. V.
" which itself has no existence, but upon the data of nature.
" In this universality of musical ideas, I hold for certain, that
" the antient modes of the Greeks agreed with our old Italian
" modes, which I must here distinguish from our present modes.
" Of these last, I shall soon give an account. The specific
" difference of the antient Greek modes consists in the precision
" of movement, which we may call the breaking of musical
" notes, according to the different value of syllables; in the pre-
" cision of choosing a certain voice in relation to grave and
" acute, which we will suppose to have been base rather than
" tenor, tenor rather than contralto, &c.; in the precision of
" certain intervals, as props or rests of the song, and of those
" lesser intervals (we may call them scales) which ought to fill
" up the greater, and to be limited to a certain extent; in
" the precision of the manner of expression, which is different
" in every different mode, (we call it taste) according to the
" nature of the passion intended to be raised; in the precision
" of a certain instrument to accompany the voice, such as
" suited the mode and the passion. These are all the dictates
" of nature; but I do not undertake to enumerate them all.
" Add to this, that amongst the Greeks the musician was joined
" to the poet, the poet to the philosopher; and that the same
" person, being musician, poet, and philosopher, treated natural
" subjects in conformity to nature, amongst a people lively,
" cultivated and interested in the subjects themselves."

Tartini, in the preceding passage, has given a most formidable § 113.
list of requisites to qualify a man to produce any thing extraor- *Unknown or despised by the moderns.*
dinary in music. If we are not to look upon our author as a
mere enthusiast, a modern composer, one would think, must be
very full of himself, who would not blush when he examines his

own

CHAP. V. own works by the rules here laid down. However, human nature is wonderfully ready at finding out reasons for self-complacency; and here the expedient is at hand; for almost every man compares himself with the rival of his own time; his ambition looks no farther; and 'tis a thousand to one, if he should deign to look backward, that he pities the ignorance or bad taste of former ages, instead of trying to gain instruction from them. But to return to my master.

§ 114.
Roman music not so perfect as the Greek.

" I am far from thinking that music passed from the Greeks
" to the Romans with the idea I have given; much less from
" the Romans to us. From thence sprung its declension and
" total destruction. What remained, amongst our old Italians, is
" only the material substance, stript of the greatest and most
" important parts of the above-mentioned precisions. That in
" the modes of the old ecclesiastical hymns is preserved faithfully,
" and with precision, the nature of the mode, according to the
" respective rules established, is certainly true; but there wants
" something more; for it is not proved, that they are the rules
" which the Greeks followed. For the rest, the movement, or
" breaking of the notes with a proper ratio, and the prosody de-
" termined for a certain effect; the determinate assignment of the
" song rather to a specific grave, than to a specific acute voice,
" and the contrary; the choice of certain intervals, rather than
" others; the expression of the song, rather in this than in that
" manner; the choice of the instrument proper for the mode; all
" these things from that time were neglected, and have never been
" thought of since. What we have added of our own are, simul-
" taneous harmony, i. e. the combination of many voices toge-
" ther; the modulation; and a fine manner or taste. As to the
" effect which our harmony can produce, in respect to the pur-
" pose of exciting the passions, I have, in my opinion, sufficiently
" proved,

" proved, that it can have none in particular, as it ought to have. CHAP. V.
" What effect our modulation can produce is now to be con-
" sidered.

" I have above distinguished the old Italian modes from our § 115.
" truly modern ones. The distinction was necessary, in regard *Modern modu-*
" to the modulation, which, as I have observed in another place, *lation.*
" and you very well understand, means the passing from the tone
" proposed to a different one; but which has relation to the tone
" first proposed. It is not sufficient, for the present purpose, to
" give a general explication; it is necessary to come to particu-
" lars, in such a manner as to convey a compleat idea of it, and
" that too scientifically; because it is an essential part of our mo-
" dern music, and therefore ought indispensably to have a place
" in this treatise. This then will be a proper place, as being
" necessary here, in order to make a comparison between the
" modes.

" The principal foundation of our modes arises from the very § 116.
" three notes of example 3, fig. 1; upon which we saw the har- *The same sub-*
" mony was founded; from whence the common diatonic scale *ject continued.*
" was deduced. The foundation is the best possible, because it
" is reduced to the numbers 6, 8, 9, 12, and therefore is a foun-
" dation common to us and the Greeks. The notes expressed
" by these numbers are, c, G, F, C. Take away the first, as not
" necessary, as being only the octave, and there remain c, G, F,
" which are supposed to be first or primary bases in the 3d major,
" as has been demonstrated in its place. To every note let its
" relative, with a 3d minor, be assigned; and all put together
" will be c, A, g, B, f, D. These six notes, deduced as was men-
" tioned, and understood as first bases, are the whole foundation
" of our modulation; which may wander and circulate through
                                                     " any

CHAP. V. "any of the above six notes, by transferring the scale and the har-
"mony of C; which, relatively to the example, is the principal
"tone proposed, and in which the harmony ought to begin and
"end; to G and F for the harmony of the 3d major, and again,
"by transferring the scale and harmony of A; the relative note
"with a 3d minor to C; into E and D, for the harmony of the
"3d minor. Hence arises in our compositions a prodigious num-
"ber of musical accidents; and therefore we deviate from the
"diatonic scale; because G and E have a diesis, or sharp, in
"the key; F and D a b molle, or a flat. By modulating in
"the afore-mentioned notes, and determining by harmonic ca-
"dences the tone arising from the scale, and from the harmony
"relative to them, the occurrence of these respective accidents,
"and the employment of them, are inevitable; and this the
"substance of our modulation. The order of it is not establish-
"ed by fixed and certain laws, and in general it is regulated
"by the sentiment of the composer; though, indeed, it may be
"said, that sentiment brings us acquainted with many truths,
"which serve afterwards for laws.

§ 117.
The passage from the principal tone to the 5th natural.

"The passing, in the modulation, from the principal tone with
"a 3d major, to the 5th of the tone, is pleasing, according to
"common sentiment; and therefore that is made a rule. This
"rule is founded on principle, and consequently can be accounted
"for. The tone with a 3d major is by its intrinsic nature har-
"monic; therefore the passage of the modulation, from the
"principal note to the 5th, is conformable to the nature of the
"harmonic scale; because the passage is from the extreme to
"the mean. From this most certain principle it happens, that
"when, by the modulation, the tone, sense, and period are once
"settled, all men, by the force of natural sentiment, feel the re-
"pugnance that occurs, in passing with the modulation from

"the

"the principal note of the tone with a 3d major, to the 4th CHAP. V.
"of the tone. This repugnance arises from the contra-
"riety of nature. The 4th of the tone divides the octave
"of the tone arithmetically. If the tone is with a 3d major,
"which is harmonic by nature, we ought to feel a repug-
"nance: If the tone is with a 3d minor, which is arithmetical
"by nature, we shall perceive no repugnance. It is true, that
"this repugnance does not arise from any defect that is in the
"original plan, or in the composer. The tone of C is composed
"of two natures, harmonic and arithmetical; and therefore the
"modulation may rightly proceed through the two means, har-
"monic and arithmetical. However, when there are in the
"same tone the two modulations, the comparison that arises
"necessarily, from their being near to one another, discovers
"the perfection of one, and the imperfection of the other, and
"makes us perceive the repugnance.

"In general, if we attend to the nature of the tone, and to § 118.
"the nearest relative notes, so that the modulation may proceed *Modulation*
"by steps, and not by jumps; (it would be, for example, *should be by easy transi-*
"a jump, and not a step, in modulation, to pass without a pro- *tions.*
"per medium from a tone with b molle to a tone with a diesis ✱,
"and the contrary); if we attend to the keeping of the modu-
"lation more in the principal tone, than in the accessory and re-
"lative tones; the contrary of which is often seen; and parti-
"cularly in a distinct manner at the beginning and end of the
"composition; with these precautions our modulation would
"be compleat. But it would lead me too far out of the way, to
"enter fully into this subject; and therefore let the general idea
"I have given suffice for the present purpose.

§ 119.
"What we find in the church-music, in the harmony, and in *Modes of the*
"the songs according to the modes of the 15th century, is very *15th century different from*
                        "different *ours.*

Chap. V.   "different from our modulation. We find there no modulation,
"but what intrinsically belongs to the tone proposed; and all
"the music of those times remains perfectly and rigorously in
"the diatonic scale; and therefore no musical accidents whatever
"are found in it, except the diesis necessary to the 7th note of
"the scale in the 3d minor, in order to form the harmonic ca-
"dence in the tone proposed; which always remains the same
"throughout the whole composition. If we compare these two
"manners of music together, we shall find, that the old Italian
"manner was graver, more majestic, and severe, than ours; ours
"more varied, and prettier. If we compare both these Italian
"manners to the antient Greek ones, I hold for certain, that
"the old Italian manner approached nearer to that of the Greeks;
"and this is easy to conclude, from what has been already said.
"Our modulation is very complex, and our ideas correspond
"with it; for, in general, the composition which has the greatest
"variety in a modulation, kept within reasonable bounds, is most
"esteemed amongst us. I must confess, that both in Italy and
"elsewhere, there are some most excellent masters in this way,
"whose skill raises my admiration, and affords me an opportu-
"nity of improving. But I doubt with reason whether or no
"this skill of theirs is conformable to nature.

§ 120.
Tasto fermo.

"Two things I have observed for some time past, with at-
"tention and reflexion. In our musical compositions, after the
"modulation has wandered about through the tones, now and
"then, towards the end, a tasto fermo is formed in the funda-
"mental base for many bars together; and upon this base the
"modulation goes on with various accompaniments, of which
"the same principal note continues to be base; and therefore
"the modulation remains in the same tone, of which the tasto
"fermo is the first base; which, for that reason, can only be
"either the 5th, or the principal note in the tone proposed.
               "Whatever

"Whatever the modulation may be, it must necessarily be ex- CHAP. V.
"tremely simple, although discordant accompaniments be inter-
"mixt; because it is finally regulated and supported by one
"single base note.

"I have observed, on various occasions, one constant effect § 121.
"from it: The same audience, which frequently gave little or *Effect of the*
"no attention to the composition, I have always seen attentive *tasto fermo.*
"to the harmony of the tasto fermo. Let this be examined,
"and, if it be found true, let it be allowed, that my observation
"is founded on nature. My other observation is common to all
"nations, where our modern music is used. Every one of these
"nations has its popular songs, many of which are of antient
"tradition, many newly composed, and adopted by common
"consent. In general, they are extremely simple; nay, it may
"be observed, that the most simple are most in vogue. It is
"certain, that in these there cannot be much modulation, at
"most in the 5th of the tone. That the people listen with greater
"pleasure to one of these songs, than to the most exquisite song
"modulated through all the maze of harmony, is an observation
"as easy to make, as it is significant when verified. But it will
"be said, the effect is equivocal, because it may as well proceed,
"and perhaps will proceed, more from the words of the song,
"which are interesting, than from the music. I answer, that
"let the same words be joined to the simple song, and to another
"exquisitely modulated, according to our art; and let the same
"musician sing both one and the other; yet still the judgment
"will certainly be in favor of the first song. I repeat what I
"have said elsewhere; nature has more power than art: and I
"add with frankness, that the greatest and best part of music
"is diatonic, but the most difficult to treat well, precisely by reason
"of its extreme simplicity, as being nearest allied to nature.
" It

CHAP. V. "If this is so, our modulation has made us deviate more from
"the end at which the Greeks aimed, than the old Italians."

§ 122.
Simple music best.
I believe most men, if they dared to speak their own feelings, would talk the language of Tartini; but the dread of being thought to have a vulgar taste, puts them under restraints, and makes them undergo the fatigue of silently listening, with a dozing kind of attention, if they are well-bred, and ashamed to interrupt others, to what they are told is fine, but which they cannot, with all their endeavours, be brought to think agreeable; whereas many of our old simple songs steal our affections, in spite of all our prejudices, and even when we are almost ashamed to be touched by such low and vulgar things; but high-bred taste, like high-born pride, is sometimes forced to listen to the humble dictates of nature, and enjoy a pleasure it dares not openly avow. Since this is the case, it is no wonder that the Beggar's Opera pleased so much at first, and still continues to be the darling of the nation; for I think there is a greater number of truly affecting songs in it, than can be picked out of many (I will not say how many) volumes of operas: But who dares own they like the music? Every body goes for the sake of Polly and Macheath, and only bear the tunes. That this should happen in our northern climate, where the ear is in general certainly not so delicate as in Italy, would neither be extraordinary, nor conclusive in favor of simple music; and therefore there wanted the express testimony of the greatest composer and performer in the climate most favorable to music, in order to convince us, that we do not judge as we do, or as I suppose we do, merely from the dullness and depravity of our organs. Let us then boldly say, with the Duke in Twelfth Night, Act II. sc. 6.

' Give me that piece of song,

' That old and antique song we heard last night;

' Methought

> ‘ Methought it did relieve my paffion much ;
> ‘ More than light airs, and recollected terms
> ‘ Of thefe more brifk and giddy-pated times.
>   ‘ It is old and plain ;
> ‘ The fpinfters, and the knitters in the fun,
> ‘ And the free maids, that weave their thread with bones,
> ‘ Do ufe to chaunt it.’

CHAP. V.

But I muft obferve, upon this occafion, that there is a mongrel kind of fongs, neither Englifh nor Italian, which rowl through a parcel of unmeaning notes, without either rhythm or melody, and are of all mufic the moft infipid; having neither the fimplicity of the old ballad, nor the delicacy of the opera ftile; which laft, for foothing the ear, is infinitely fuperior to what is known in any other nation.

" There remains to be confidered, what effects, in order to attain the fame purpofe of exciting the fame paffions as the Greeks did, our fine manner, or what is called good tafte, can produce. This confifts firft and principally in the voice of the finger, now lengthened and held out with fweetnefs, now lowered or pufhed out with force, or fuftained, according as the paffage requires, &c. 2dly, In appogiatura's, trills, modes of breaking the time, either by fhortening or protracting, modes of finging either natural or artificial, adapted to what the fong requires, &c. But, before I proceed farther in my fubject, I muft caution you not to imagine I go upon a falfe fuppofition, as it may appear that I fuppofe good tafte to be an invention of our times. I own, it is neither an invention of modern nor of antient times; it is the product of human nature. From the time that there was finging and playing, nature itfelf, independently of art, has caufed extraordinary productions in every age and every country; and will

§ 123.
Good tafte.

CHAP. V. " will continue to exert her privilege of doing the same, as long
" as the world and the human species endure. Hence art was
" derived; and I am certain that there has been, and must be,
" good taste, relative I mean to times and musical modes, as an
" essential part of music, so far as the execution is concerned.
" My proposition refers to our times, and our musical modes,
" and therefore is particular. If our mode of music is different
" from the antient Italian modes, in proportion our good taste
" ought to be different from that of our ancestors: If it were
" otherwise, there must be a very essential and great error in one
" of the two; it being utterly impossible, not only in nature, but
" in art, that, two different species of music being supposed,
" the same expression and modification can agree with both.
" The thing is so clear, that it would be lost time to prove it.
" But upon good taste depend expression and modification, and
" these ought to be different: Therefore good taste must be
" different. I do not say, that its first and general principles
" ought not to be uniform, in every mode of music whatever.
" A voice excellent by nature, and perfectly well regulated, is
" an universal principle; and, when nature is defective, the as-
" sistance of art becomes necessary; because, in my opinion,
" the universality and the greatest perfection of good taste con-
" sists in the voice and expression. This I call true good taste,
" according to nature; because it agrees with every mode of
" music whatever. Every thing else is particular, to such a de-
" gree, that when we examine, without prejudice, the propriety
" or impropriety of the use of trills, appogiatura's, cantabile
" manner, &c. there will be found many cases, in which none
" of these things can reasonably be used."

§ 124.   I cannot help breaking in upon my author, in his excellent
Abuse of taste. and truly sensible observations upon true taste; a thing so little
understood,

[87]

understood, that people are very apt to imagine, that it is the same in all the different modes of music; the contrary to which is clearly true; but I break in upon him, in order to prove how necessary it is to make the distinction he has made, in order to get rid of a very extraordinary innovation, lately introduced, of bringing the Italian manner into our old English ballads; which I am told, for I did not choose to hear such an unnatural mixture myself, was practised on our stage; but, absurd as this may be, Tartini will soon give us an instance, which will shew the rage of good taste full as strongly; for he continues, and says,

CHAP. V.

" In our churches, the Miserere mei Deus is performed; and
" on the stage heroes and heroines go to death with the very finest
" musical graces above mentioned. It is well that custom and
" habit do not give room for reflexion; however, very little re-
" flexion is sufficient to turn all the pleasure, that can be re-
" ceived from the most perfect execution, immediately into its
" contrary. The song adapted to the passion, the voice adapted
" to the song, both as to its natural quality, and as to the act of
" modification, as well as to its pitch, will always prevail, in
" every time and in every circumstance. This is all that can
" be called general. If we descend to particulars, I understand
" very well the propriety of adapting our musical graces to a
" great number of songs; but of the adapting of those graces
" to all songs, I understand nothing, nor ever shall. I am too
" much persuaded and convinced, that, in order to have a song
" truly adapted to the passion that is expressed by the words,
" every song ought to have its individual and particular modes
" of expression, and, in consequence, its individual and specific
" good taste. That the Greeks understood and practised in this
" manner was absolutely necessary for their intent; a proposi-
" tion so true, in my opinion, that, had they acted otherwise,
" I would.

§ 125.
Abuse of good taste.

Chap. V. " I would deny the fact, the history, and the possibility in na-
" ture. If we understand and act otherwise, the reason is, that
" music alone, and separated from any other consideration what-
" ever, is become our only aim and intention. This being pro-
" posed as genus, species, and individual, and every thing being
" referred to that alone, our harmony, our songs, and our good
" taste do exceedingly well. In this sense, we have, here and
" elsewhere, most excellent composers and performers, whose
" skill pleases and suits the genius of all Europe; a most certain
" sign, in general, that this is right in nature, for nemo omnes
" fallit. But, if the same end was proposed as that which the
" Greeks had in view, we are very far from a possibility of ob-
" taining it with the means we use. Our harmony is in oppo-
" sition, as including different species of grave and acute: In
" order to obtain their intention, one species only, individually
" belonging to the passion, must be employed. Our song is in
" opposition, as being modulated according to our art; as being
" unconfined by any reference to prosody, either in matter or in
" form; as not being obliged to choose intervals of a greater or
" less extent, as to high or low, nor tied down to the choice of
" a determinate voice.

§ 126. " If we would therefore pursue the same end which the Greeks
How the pas- " did, we should act quite contrary to what we do; we should
sions are to be " make use of one principal tone only; we should regulate our
moved. " music by our prosody, as to long and short syllables, and
" particularly in respect to metrical feet proper for the passion;
" a thing as necessary as it is difficult; to which feet the song
" ought to correspond identically: We should use with precision
" certain intervals chosen with analogy to the nature of the pas-
" sion; (necessary also, but difficult;) we should use a determi-
" nate extent of notes, as to grave and acute; and also a specific
" voice,

"voice, rather grave than acute, rather in the middle than the
"extreme; or the contrary, according to the nature of the
"passion. But lastly, our good taste is in opposition to the end
"the Greeks proposed, as being just the same in every song
"whatever, and as being formed of such component parts as
"carry with them an evident contradiction to nature, when ap-
"plied to all circumstances without distinction. Whereas good
"taste ought to vary perpetually, according to the different
"passions; and should be composed of such minute component
"parts, as are specific and individual to the particular mode of
"song required by the passion, and never transferrable to any
"other mode. If the passion is mixt with other passions, as
"frequently happens, in that case there is one generally princi-
"pal and predominant, and this must be the chief object. If
"two passions are equal in degree, which is possible, then in the
"same song the object of the composer will be doubled, in pro-
"portion to the force of the two different passions.

"I am entering too far into this affair before I am aware;
"not too far, because I doubt of the truth of the foregoing pro-
"positions; but because, great as the obscurity of this affair
"may be, they appear to me to result with so much precision,
"that if you, my noble friend, were to require of me a musical
"example, deduced from them, it would be thought, that you
"would have more reason to require it than I to deny it. But
"softly, I beseech; my propositions are deduced from observa-
"tion upon nature, common to the Greeks and us; and there-
"fore are deduced from the first of all sources. Their precision
"therefore does not intrinsically arise from their deduction, but
"from their adaption to the antient and modern modes compared
"together. A precision of such a kind is not sufficient for the
"purpose of exhibiting an example; a great deal more is want-
"ing;

CHAP. V.

§ 127. *The difficulty of moving the passions.*

CHAP. V. "ing; a conjunction of three things in one is required; an habitual
"and specific knowledge of the passions, skill in music, and talents
"for poetry; and therefore a philosopher, a musician, and a poet,
"each eminent in his way, are necessary.

§ 128.
The same considered.
"But, besides the foregoing requisites, a disposition in the audi-
"ence, in general, to feel the effect is necessary; and also in par-
"ticular, in different respects, as the being accustomed to such a
"kind of music; for I am certain, that, without this, the ablest
"musician, that ever was among the Greeks, might sing his best,
"without producing any effect, before a Dalmatian audience,
"whose music has no determinate intervals, but consists in a con-
"tinued effort of the voice in grave and acute, merely discretion-
"ary. 2dly, Conformity of ideas in respect to manner; for
"if the ideas of the hearer are not conformable to the manner
"represented, he will either remain indifferent, or, if they are
"contrary, instead of being delighted, he will be offended. I
"am certain, if an object of the most tragical nature was repre-
"sented before a cannibal, he would not be shocked, but would
"enjoy it. 3dly, A conformity of movement to the metre: For
"there are people, and whole nations, whose movements are by
"nature slow; others, whose movements are quick; others tem-
"perate, or moderate. That movement, which is not able to
"stir one man, will be more than sufficient to stir another; this
"is the case in general, in relation to nature and education. In
"particular, as to nature and education, whoever is sufficiently
"acquainted with the nations of Europe only, must have ob-
"served the difference of movement amongst different countries,
"during the intense influence of each respective passion."

§ 129.
The same continued.
"These differences are, each by itself, generical, and generical
"in the highest degree; out of all which, a species being formed,
"one

" one might perhaps be able to compose a proper example; I CHAP. V.
" say perhaps, because, in respect to the union of all the above-
" mentioned conditions, which composed the genus of the an-
" tient Greeks, though we should be able to discover and execute
" it, just as it was amongst that people, I much doubt whether
" it would produce with us the same effect." One may guess,
from these doctrines of our author, why he never composed any
vocal music, which I always wondered at, till I read his trea-
tises; for that touching sweetness and delicacy of stile, that variety with simplicity, which reign in a sovereign degree in all
his pieces, seemed to qualify him, above all men, for moving
the passions, particularly of the sprightly and gentle kind; and
his masterly notes would have received infinite advantage by being
joined to proper words.

" I think I have delivered nothing but what is exactly true, § 130.
" if so my doubt is reasonable; nay, if I should advance the *The same con-*
" following proposition, That it is impossible that the manners, *tinued.*
" the poetry, and the music, that were homogeneous and proper
" to the Greeks, should be equally so to us Italians, and other
" nations of our times and manners; this proposition would not
" be rash. The seeds of the passions are, in general, the same
" in all men; their specific difference arises from education and
" custom. In our case, we want not the genus, but the differ-
" ence: For this reason therefore, in the universal source of na-
" ture, our business must be much rather to search out for homoge-
" niety and propriety, relative to our present circumstances, than
" to endeavour to discover, what, if really discovered, would be
" very likely not to succeed. So much in relation to the uni-
" versal genus of all those things, which are necessary to attain
" such a purpose as was mentioned above. I have meddled more
" in

Chap. V. " in this affair than I ought, considering that the part I have un-
" dertaken is that of a musician, not of a philosopher or a poet.

§ 131.
Difference of musical intervals.

" But you, my noble friend, are waiting for me, on return-
" ing to my own profession, in order to ask my opinion in the
" concrete, and in precision, about the difference of the nature
" of our musical intervals; which I asserted above to be different
" in their nature. This is an inquiry belonging to the musician;
" and perhaps you may inquire farther, What my opinion is
" of the particular nature of the breakings or divisions of our
" musical notes, in relation identically to the value of feet in
" prosody; a consideration common, not only to the musician
" and the poet, but to the philosopher also.

§ 132.
Difficulty of ascertaining their effect.

" The first inquiry, though indeed it comes within my parti-
" cular sphere, is to me much more difficult than the second,
" which is of a common nature. The reason is obvious: The
" habits contracted by a professor accustomed to a kind of music,
" begun and continued without particular reflexions, naturalise
" to such a degree its parts, that, when there is no specific dif-
" ference between them, it is almost impossible to distinguish
" them by sentiment; much more so, if the distinction falls upon
" individuals of the same species, or parts of the same category,
" as the consonant intervals of the hexachord, and the intervals
" of the common diatonic scale. Add to this, that, as sentiment
" in all men is not perfectly the same, and uniform, no conclu-
" sion can be drawn from it; on the contrary, being individual
" and particular, it does not produce that certainty which is ne-
" cessary to constitute science. We must therefore search spe-
" cifically in what particulars the sentiment of all mankind is
" common and uniform; and generically endeavour to find out
" a prin-

"a principle of univerſal reaſon, which, to the diſgrace of par- CHAP. V.
"ticular prejudices contracted, may correct our ſentiment, if
"need be; and, to the diſgrace of cuſtom, render it aſſured
"and enlightened. This is no ſmall matter to bring about,
"nor is it indifferent. But to the trial.

"In order to act, as I ought, conſiſtently with my principles, § 133.
"the examination of ſentiment and reaſon ought to fall upon *Of the diffe-*
"the harmony, and not the ſong; becauſe the harmony is the *rent nature of the 3d major*
"cauſe and foundation, the ſong is the effect and offspring *and minor.*
"According to the common ſentiment of all thoſe nations where
"our muſic is cultivated, the harmony of the 3d major is ſtrong,
"lively, bold; the harmony of the 3d minor is languid, me-
"lancholy, and ſoft. Upon bringing this common ſentiment
"to the teſt of reaſon, no other cauſe of a phyſical and demon-
"ſtrative kind can be aſſigned, but the harmonic nature of the
"3d major, and the arithmetical nature of the 3d minor; the
"firſt being continuous, and therefore ſtronger; the laſt, con-
"tiguous only, and therefore more languid. From the force
"of the 3d major ariſes the lively and bold effect; from the
"weakneſs of the 3d minor, the melancholy and gentle effect.

"Reflecting on this principle, derived from reaſon, I find, § 134.
"that a paſſage of the 4th aſcending ought to have more force *Aſcending and*
"than the ſame paſſage deſcending, on account of the harmonic *deſcending in-*
"cadence formed by the aſcending paſſage; of the arithmetical *tervals.*
"cadence formed by the deſcending. In vertu of this reaſon, I
"obſerve what happens to myſelf, and make others obſerve how
"it happens to them; and find that my own ſentiment, and that
"of others, correſpond to the reaſon aſſigned; and it is agreed
"that thus it happens in nature. The ſame reaſon, therefore,
"will hold good for the deſcending and aſcending 5ths: De-
                    "ſcending,

CHAP. V. "scending, they will be more forceable, chearful, and bold;
"descending, more feeble, melancholy, and soft; because, in
"descending, they form an harmonic cadence, in ascending, an
"arithmetical one: Therefore, in a progression of ascending
"5ths, in the fundamental base, the harmony will be strong
"and lively, of descending 5ths the contrary, &c.

§ 135.
Some subject continued.
"As the progression of the above-mentioned passage sets the
"effect in a stronger light; so let any number of professors give
"their judgment, and I will venture to affirm, that it will be
"conformable to reason. The same may be said of a progres-
"sion of 5ths. But progression makes a song, and the part
"follows the nature of the whole: Therefore, songs formed from
"the progression of passages above-mentioned, will be respec-
"tively of the same nature: Therefore, by means of this prin-
"ciple, one may discover the nature of every interval in the
"diatonic scale; because, if from the progression of the har-
"mony the song arises, and this cannot but be of the same na-
"ture with the harmony from whence it arises; then the hemi-
"tone major, and the tone minor, both demonstratively ascend-
"ing, being given upon the harmonic cadence, the effect of
"them, as ascending, will be strong, cheerful, bold. Change
"now the harmonic cadence into the arithmetical, in which case
"the aforesaid same intervals, and same notes, will demonstra-
"tively descend; and the effect of them, as descending, will
"be languid, melancholy, and soft. But of the vivacity and
"force of the hemitone major ascending, and of the softness of
"the same note descending, we are convinced, to the reproach
"of custom; and the tone minor, that is over the hemitone, is
"physically demonstrative of the same harmony: Therefore,
"that such is the nature of these two intervals, appears both
"by reason and sentiment."

If

If I underſtand my author, he means this: Suppoſe the chord E *g* is followed by the chord F *a*; then it is clear, that the baſe is *c* F, as he has put it in the example, and the 5th deſcends, which, according to the foregoing doctrine, is of a ſtrong and lively nature. Suppoſe, on the other hand, the chord F *a* to precede the chord E *c*; then the baſe will be F *c*, i. e. an aſcending 5th, which, he ſays, is of a melancholy and languid nature. Now that the baſe is F *c*, is clear from the phænomenon of the 3d ſounds, to ſay nothing more; for F *a*, being a 3d major, has for 3d ſound the octave of F, or the loweſt note in the chord; and E *c*, being a 3d minor, has for baſe the tenth lower than the loweſt note in the chord, i. e. C.

§ 136. *Explication of the foregoing article.*

This whole doctrine about the effect of intervals, as far as I know, is entirely new, and of great conſequence; but I muſt frankly confeſs, that in ſome reſpects I do not perfectly agree with Tartini. He lays the whole ſtreſs upon the harmonic and arithmetical cadences: I think, the effect often depends on paſſing from the extreme to the mean, or the contrary, which difference will, I beli.ve, anſwer in many caſes; but then we muſt take in another conſideration, which I wonder he ſhould omit, as he has been ſo accurate and explicit about the effect of bars. Now I am apt to imagine, that the melancholy effect, or the contrary, does not depend barely upon the harmonic or arithmetical cadence, or on going from the extreme to the mean, or the contrary; but alſo upon the place where the extreme or mean falls in the bar. Thus, let us take theſe notes, C, G, E, C, and let the bar begin with the firſt C, I have no doubt but that they will have a lively effect. Take now the ſame notes in the ſame order, and let the bar begin upon G, and I imagine their effect will be totally changed. But I go farther, and maintain, that though,

§ 137. *This doctrine about intervals new.*

CHAP. V.

CHAP. V. though the 3d minor is of a melancholy nature in general, yet let the ictus fall upon the extreme, and the soft and melancholy effect will disappear. Again, take the same notes, and let the ictus fall upon the mean, and a quite contrary effect will be produced; the air will be soft and languid. For it must be observed, that the 3d minor is full as well adapted to express rage and violence, arising from grief, despair, &c. as melancholy of the gentle kind; and that the 3d major is not only adapted to express cheerfulness, anger, and indignation, but also serenity, and composed tenderness. I could give instances, to confirm the doctrine above delivered, out of opera songs; but I choose rather to leave the whole to be considered by musicians of taste and feeling, who cannot be at a loss to find examples of all the kinds. Let us return to Tartini.

§ 138.
Effect of the octave.

"Here then we have got a key to lay open the nature of in-
"tervals by the force of reason; this key is the harmony; and
"therefore the hardest interval to account for is the principal
"interval of all; I mean the octave; because it cannot be refer-
"red to the harmony. We must therefore examine it in another
"light. Since this is the chief of all the intervals, its character
"must be simple, grave, and majestic. Its character of sim-
"plicity is manifest by the conversion of the acute term into the
"grave, because it becomes unisonous. Its gravity and ma-
"jesty appear to me as manifest, inasmuch as it cannot, by its
"nature, be proper for any part but the base; and therefore it
"is an interval strong and severe, though joined to the utmost
"simplicity. In fact, a song filled with many progressive in-
"tervals of the octave, either ascending or descending, and exe-
"cuted along with corresponding notes by a base and a soprano,
"(extremes set off one another best); when it is well executed
"by a base, will impose and produce the aforesaid excellent ef-
"fect;

"effect; if well executed by a soprano, it will not only not pro- CHAP. V.
"duce the same effect, but it will be difgustful and shocking."

"Here begins to open another principle of reason and senti- § 139.
"timent, which is the agreement of intervals with the voice. *Intervals in*
"Rigorously speaking, the principle is the same, *viz.* harmony; *relation to the voice.*
"but as in harmony, disposed strictly according to rule, every
"interval has its particular place in the respective voices, that in-
"tegrate or constitute harmony; so in proportion as in the progres-
"sion of the harmony, the song is formed by the voices, the in-
"tervals which result necessarily, and not arbitrarily, arise re-
"spectively individuated to every voice; and this is the particu-
"lar principle of their agreement. In relation therefore to these
"two principles, the consideration is twofold, in every interval
"of the diatonic scale, i. e. both as to the nature of the effect,
"and as to the agreement of the place. The consequences and
"deductions from hence are such and so many, that they are
"equivalent to an entire and ample treatise. But this is not a
"place to treat upon them; and you, my noble friend, know
"very well how to do it yourself.

"I proceed therefore to give you my opinion on the nature § 140.
"of breaking musical notes, with reference to the value of feet *Breaking of*
"in prosody; I mean really the nature of the feet, and not the *notes.*
"nature of the musical notes; because, in this respect, music is
"subservient to poetry. This affair belongs properly to the poet,
"much more in the character of a philosopher than a musician.
"The thing is clear, because the business of a philosopher is to
"search out what kind of movement is adapted to each passion,
"and therefore he ought to know immediately the correspon-
"dence of the internal and external senses; which will enable
"him to open his way to the internal senses, by means of external
"movements

Chap. V. "movements properly adapted. The musician has nothing to
"do but to preserve the above-mentioned movements with exact-
"ness and rigor; I therefore said before, that the first inquiry
"about the nature of musical intervals was to me much more
"difficult than the second, about the way of breaking the in-
"tervals. In the first inquiry, it was my duty to interest myself,
"and thoroughly enter into it as a musician; in the second,
"I am not concerned, as being neither poet nor philosopher.
"Produce me then a poet, who is also a philosopher, and will
"perform his part, and in this case I think certainly, that I, even
"I, should be able to perform mine. This is my opinion about
"the second inquiry.

§ 141.
Music and dancing go together.

"Were you however, who have so much power over me, to insist
"upon my making trial of myself as poet and philosopher, upon
"this subject; I will tell you, with my usual sincerity, that by
"word of mouth I shall have no difficulty to declare my senti-
"ments to you in private, as freely as you can desire or command;
"in writing, certainly not. I know my limits, and observe them
"rigorously. Nothing is more easy than the communication of
"what is written, either by reading or by a copy; and I blush
"already at the thoughts of appearing as a musician, poet, and
"philosopher. I have undertaken more than enough, as a musi-
"cian only; insomuch that I am rather confounded, than satis-
"fied, with what I have already done. Let this be my utmost
"boundary; or, if I presume to go one step farther on this sub-
"ject, let it be to make a particular malicious observation. It
"is this: Wherever there is music (and music there is, of some
"sort or other, in every nation) it is never found without
"dancing. This is a key to discover and deduce movements,
"and musical breaks, relative to the diversity of people; nor is
"there any danger of being led into an error by attending to it,

"as

"as it is the very language of nature. From hence arises that
" conſtancy, for ages, in the uſe of the ſame kind of dance,
" adopted by each nation reſpectively, to ſuch a degree, that at
" laſt dances get their name from the nation where they are prac-
" tiſed. In each of theſe dances, we ſhall infallibly find the
" phyſical movements correſponding with the long and ſhort
" ſyllables, and metrical feet; it is ſufficient to obſerve and
" make uſe of them, which is no difficult matter. You have
" my philoſophy on this point, which I call by a more proper
" name, a malicious obſervation. Do you, illuſtrious Sir, judge
" whether, in the preſent caſe, it is better to be a philoſopher
" or an obſerver. Here I put an end to the 5th chapter, much
" better pleaſed with myſelf for having obeyed you, than for
" having written what I have."

CHAP. V.

Before I enter upon an examination of Tartini's next chapter, I ſhall give the ſyſtem of the 3d minor, which I promiſed § 44, and which I choſe to place here, as the knowledge of it is particularly neceſſary for underſtanding the remaining part of his book: But as I have not hitherto fully explained the foundation of the ſyſtem of the 3d major, or, at leaſt, have not put it in a point of light, which will ſerve to explain the ſyſtem of the 3d minor, I ſhall begin firſt with that.

§ 142.
3d minor

It was obſerved, § 53, that Tartini, in order to fill up the oc-tave, made uſe of the muſical intervals C, F, G, C, expreſſed by the numbers 6, 8, 9, 12, which Pythagoras is ſuppoſed to have firſt diſcovered, vide § 12. Why thoſe notes only can be uſed as baſes, ſhall now be made evident. No notes then can be prime baſes, but ſuch as have perfect 3ds major and perfect 5ths belonging to them; for this is the preciſe and ſpecific idea fur-niſhed by the ſtring of three ſounds, § 2. With theſe the ear

§ 143.
3d major

CHAP. V. is satisfied, and with none else; and what Aristoxenus says, p. 33, is certainly true, though misapplied by him, that the sensation of a musical ear may be almost looked upon as a first principle in music. Let us now examine the notes of the octave by the rule above-mentioned.

$$\begin{array}{ll} \text{C has for} & \left\{ \begin{array}{l} \text{3d, E perfect.} \\ \text{5th, G perfect.} \end{array} \right. \\ \text{D } - - & \text{3d, F imperfect.} \\ \text{E } - - & \text{3d, G imperfect.} \\ \text{F } - - & \left\{ \begin{array}{l} \text{3d, A perfect.} \\ \text{5th, C perfect.} \end{array} \right. \\ \text{G } - - & \left\{ \begin{array}{l} \text{3d, B perfect.} \\ \text{5th, D perfect.} \end{array} \right. \\ \text{A } - - & \text{3d, C imperfect.} \\ \text{B } - - & \text{3d, D imperfect.} \end{array}$$

From hence it appears, that there can be but three prime bases, viz. C, F, and G, in the diatonic octave.

§ 144.
3d *major*.

From the foregoing observation it appears also, that all other notes besides C, F, and G, when used as bases, must have some figure or figures belonging to them; which figure or figures, when put over them, shew that such bases are not prime or fundamental; and at the same time give the true base; so that all of them together make 3d and 5th. Thus to go through the notes of the octave, C, F, and G, have no figure over them; because 3d and 5th are played with them of course. D ought to have $^4_6$ over it, which shew that it is not prime base. Now, the 4th to D is G, and the 6th to D is B; so that, as it appeared before, that B cannot be a prime base, G must be so in this case. Now, B, D, make 3d and 5th to G. Next, E ought to have 6 over it; therefore C, which is 6th to E, is prime base; and these two notes, along with the 3d to E, which is always supposed when the 4th is not marked, give the 3d and 5th to C. G ought to have $^6_4$ over it for the same reason that D has: For though it is sometimes a prime base, yet as in regularly ascending through the notes of the octave, it goes immediately before a close in F, it must be considered here as 5th of C. Next, A ought to have 6 over it, for the same reason that E has. Lastly, B ought to have 6 over it, for the same reason; so that the notes of the octave, used as bases, stand thus, along with the correspondent prime bases:

CHAP. V.

	$^6_4$	6		$^6_4$	6	6
C	D	E	F	G	A	B	C.
C	G	C	F	C	F	G	C.

Let us now proceed to the investigation of the system of the 3d minor, which I shall do in a way different from what Tartini takes, but still making use of his clue. He observes, that there is a note arising in the hexachord, which he marks E$^\flat$, fig. 1. ex. 3. This note is a 3d minor to C, the fundamental and universal base to all the notes in the hexachord. Here then is a beginning given to a system very different from that of the common diatonic scale. I have shewn § 40, that this note is a consonance, as every note in the hexachord, whether it be arithmetical or harmonic, must be; as they all arise from aliquot parts of 60; and I have besides given, § 41, some reason to think that all these notes do, potentially at least, if not actually, exist as sounds, upon striking a musical string; nay, that they do sometimes exist actually, I shall endeavour to prove afterwards. But, however this may be, we certainly have got a beginning for the system of the 3d minor, in the most natural, and, I may say, the only natural, way: For whatever system, as Tartini observes, does not arise from the harmonic, must be arbitrary. To which I will add, that to suppose any thing to be arbitrary, which is universally pleasing,

§ 145. *3d minor.*

CHAP. V. pleasing, is to suppose that our senses were framed without any specific adaption to the objects that affect them; and that in some particulars only, when in others of the same kind we can trace the utmost regularity; which is a supposition too wild to be admitted.

§ 146.
Investigation of the 3d minor.
But to quit theory, and come to experiment. Let any musician, after having fully settled the tone of C with a 3d major, descend from C through G, F, E, to E^b, and he will find, that he is brought out of the system of the 3d major into that of the 3d minor imperceptibly and agreeably; and that he may, if he pleases, by playing D after E^b, make a close in C. In this case, he is got full into the system of the 3d minor; but how to continue in it is the difficulty. This difficulty, great as it is, I will now endeavour to solve, expecting the indulgence of the reader, if I fail, in a point which has never, as far as I know, been cleared up satisfactorily; not even by Tartini himself; though he has established the true scale, and the right use of it, by a very instructive example, and also furnished every principle I make use of in this intricate affair. In order to understand it, I desire the reader to recollect what was said, § 143, about the necessity of having 3ds major and 5ths to every prime base; but we must except the 3d to C, in this case, from the very nature of the thing. We have got therefore C, E^b, G; but, in order to make a full close upon C, its 5th, or G, must have 3d major and 5th; i. e. B and D. We have therefore got B, C, D, E^b, G. Again, the 3d found to C, E^b, is A^b; vide fig. 3: Therefore only one note, viz. between E^b and G, is wanting to compleat the octave. Let us suppose it to be F, then the 3d found to F, A^b, will be D^b; but D was settled, as well as A^b: Therefore, since A^b, which, along with F, produced D^b, (which cannot belong to the scale) cannot be

be altered, F neceſſarily muſt. Let us make F✱ 3d major to CHAP. V.
D, and the 3d found to F✱, A♭, is B, which belongs to the
ſcale. I might as well have determined F✱ by the 3d ſounds to
D, F and D, F✱. In the former caſe, it is B♭, which cannot
belong to the ſcale; in the latter, it is D, which does belong to
it. I muſt obſerve, upon this occaſion, that though the 3d ſounds,
belonging to the ſyſtem of the 3d minor, if heard, would be extremely diſagreeable, as being double, and their progreſſion auk-
ward, yet they always belong to the key; as will be evident at
once, to any one who examines them. We have now got all the
notes belonging to the ſyſtem of the 3d minor; becauſe, by
changing any note, we change the relation it bears to every other
note, and conſequently change the ſyſtem : Therefore F and B♭
are excluded.

§ 147.
Baſes in the 3d minor.

Let us next examine, which notes of this ſcale can be prime
baſes. D cannot, becauſe D, A♭ makes an imperfect 5th; E
cannot, becauſe B makes a ſuperfluous 5th with it; F✱ cannot,
becauſe it makes a defective 5th with C; G may be prime, becauſe
it has a perfect 3d and 5th; A♭ may be alſo prime, for the ſame
reaſon; B cannot, becauſe it makes a 3d minor with D; C is
prime of courſe : So that all the prime baſes are C, A♭, G. I
have by means of this theory, which is chiefly borrowed from
Tartini, and by the help of his muſical example in the 3d minor,
given a ſcale with the baſe, vide fig. 9. It appears by that ſcale,
that the paſſage from B to A♭, G, F✱, and from A♭ to G, F✱,
E♭, are perfectly regular.

§ 148.
Objection.

It will be ſaid, by way of objection to the ſcale above-mentioned, that no piece of muſic is to be found, where the notes,
therein ſpecified as belonging to the ſyſtem of the 3d minor, are
alone employed. I readily own that it will be difficult to find
ſuch

CHAP. V. such a piece: but yet passages of that kind are to be met with here and there in the best Italian composers, though the practice is not steady and uniform. This is not extraordinary when there is a want of principles to direct: Nor would it be extraordinary if no such passage was to be met with at all: since, as Ptolemy rightly observes, Harm. page 2: 'the senses discover what is nearly 'true, and receive from reason what is accurately so; whereas 'reason receives from the senses what is nearly true, and dis-'covers what is accurately so.' And afterwards, page 3: 'A 'man might think a circle made by the eye only to be very accu-'rate, till he has seen one made by a pair of compasses; so it is 'with the ear in music.' For this reason too much pains and study can never be employed in order to discover principles in every branch of knowledge; I mean when the pains and study are proportioned to the dignity of the subject.

§ 149.
Deviations in practice.
But the deviation from the scale above-mentioned, is not always owing to want of principles; on the contrary it is frequently owing to a change of key, which, though not attended to, is real. The tone of the 3d above, and that of the 3d below, i. e. of E^b and A^b, are so closely connected with it, that we are perpetually led by nature to touch upon one or other of them; and whenever that happens, the 4th or 7th must be altered respectively. But that happens whenever the 3d or 6th of the principal is in the beginning or middle of the bar: i. e. when they are accented. I will not affirm, that no change ought to be made in any other case; but I do not at present recollect one, where there ought to be any; and leave that point, as well as many others, to be decided by proper judges. I will say thus much, however, from my own feeling, that by substituting B and F*, in the room of B^b and F, in many places, in songs and other pieces, the effect was greatly improved.

I shall

I shall make a few observations on the aforesaid scale. 1st, § CHAP. V.
then, there are no two whole tones, following one another,
throughout the octave. This was one of the characteristics of § 150.
the antient chromatic, vide § 83. 2dly, There are two tetra- *Observation*
chords; viz. from F♯ to B, and from E♭ to A♭; consisting *on the 3d mi-*
each of two dieses; which, both together, are less than the un- *nor.*
compounded triemitone. This is another characteristic of the
antient chromatic; Aristid. p. 18; Euclid, p. 10. 3dly, The
nature of the 3d minor is soft and melancholy, which is another
characteristic of the antient chromatic. Many testimonies might
be produced in proof of this assertion; but I shall content myself
with two only at present: Aristides, p. 111, says, the chromatic
is very pleasing and plaintive; and Plutarch, Vol. II. p. 109,
puts this query, Why does the chromatic soften the mind? But
I do not conclude, from these resemblances, that they are the
same; on the contrary, I am certain they are not, both from what
Tartini has said, and from other reasons. 4thly, This system,
when practised in all its purity, is adapted to express not only
softness and melancholy, as I observed above, but peculiarly also
the conflict of jarring passions of the plaintive kind; as love
mixed with despair, jealousy, &c. The perpetual contrast of
great and small intervals, contributes, I imagine, very much
to produce this effect.

I shall now give what I promised § 60, viz. the method of § 151.
tuning the Harp for the 3d minor; which is as follows: From *Tuning the*
C to G, and from G to D, perfect 5ths; from G to B, upwards, *Harp for the*
a perfect 3d major; from B to F♯, upwards, a perfect 5th; *3d minor.*
from G to E♭, downwards, a perfect 3d major; from E♭ to A♭,
downwards, a perfect 5th: For accidental notes, from C to F,
downwards, a perfect 5th; from E♭ to B♭, upwards, a perfect
P   5th.

CHAP. V. 5th. These are the principal accidents; the rest must be managed as shall be found most expedient upon trial. I must observe, upon this occasion, how necessary it is for harpers to be particularly careful about tuning their instrument accurately; as the possibility of doing it is the chief circumstance that gives it a superiority over some other instruments; and a great advantage that is.

§ 152. I quoted before, § 62, many passages from English writers, that seemed to put the Harp on a very respectable footing. I shall now quote an express proof in its favor from a foreigner, and one who I should imagine was no bad judge of such matters, both as a theorist and a practitioner. His name is Thom. de Pinedo. Of his skill in the theory of music, he has left us a very sufficient specimen, in his notes upon Stephanus de Urbibus; where he has inserted a short dissertation on music, which is very well put together; in which are these words: 'I was incited to
' give an account of musical intervals, by the learned dissertation
' of Joan. Albert. Bannus; in which he desires some one will
' give a new constitution of music, by placing hemitones between
' all the tones, so that the art of music may be rendered compleat, and fit to move the passions. I will gratify his desire,
' which I am enabled to do by my skill on the Harp with two
' rows of strings, the QUEEN of all musical instruments; in which,
' on account of the number of its strings, viz. 39, may be seen,
' as in a glass, all the musical intervals; and by whose sweet
' harmony, arising from the discordant agreement of strings,
' struck with the fingers instead of a plectrum, I have long not
' only amused myself, but have also relieved the misery attending an undeserved banishment from my native country.'
Artic. Timoth.

Pinedo on the Harp.

I pro-

I promised likewise, § 65, to say something more of Æolus's
Harp, that extraordinary instrument invented by Father Kircher,
as extraordinary a man, who was made up of whim and genius.
The wonderful effect of this instrument has been felt by all who
have heard it, and have an ear for music. It has produced two
elegant poems in our language, and afforded an opportunity for
imagination to display itself in terms though strong, yet not
exaggerated. I shall quote one of them at length; and I pitch
upon it, in preference to the other, because it gives a compleat
idea of the great variety of music produced by a few simple unison
strings, and because it tends very much to illustrate and confirm
my theory; vide § 39, &c.

Chap. V.
§ 153.
Æolus's Harp.

ODE on ÆOLUS's HARP:
Dodsley's Miscell. Vol. III. p. 211.

1.

Æthereal race, inhabitants of air!
   Who hymn your God amid the secret grove;
Ye unseen beings, to my Harp repair,
   And raise majestic strains, or melt in love.

2.

Those tender notes, how unkindly they upbraid,
   With what soft throe they thrill the lover's heart!
Sure from the hand of some unhappy maid,
   Who dy'd of love, those sweet complainings part.

3.

But hark! that strain was of a graver tone;
   On the deep strings his hand some hermit throws;
Or he, the *sacred bard!* who sat alone
   In the drear waste, and wept his people's woes.

CHAP. V.

4.

Such was the song which Zion's children sung,
   When by Euphrates' stream they made their plaint;
And to such sadly solemn notes are strung
   Angelic Harps, to sooth a dying saint.

5.

Methinks I hear the full celestial choir
   Through heav'n's high dome their awful anthems raise;
Now chanting clear, and now they all conspire
   To swell the lofty hymn from praise to praise.

6.

Let me, ye wand'ring spirits of the wind,
   Who, as wild fancy prompts you, touch the string,
Smit with your theme, be in your chorus join'd;
   For till you cease, my muse forgets to sing.

§ 154.
Its effect not accounted for.
In the foregoing Ode, effects are described, and I think very truly, which cannot be accounted for by the common system: For the harmonic notes are only 3d, 5th, and 8th to the principal; which seem to make but one sound, as appears by adding 12th and 17th to the pipes of an organ; vide § 6. It is true, other intervals are produced, as 6th major and minor, 4th and 3d minor. But these will not account for the phænomena; whereas, if we add the arithmetical notes, the number and nature of the intervals is greatly altered. The number is 19; among which are 7ths, 6ths major and minor, 5ths, 4ths, 3ds major and minor, a tone major and a minor, a hemitone major and a minor. But it will be asked, How should these notes be heard in Æolus's Harp, when they never have been heard on a single string? I answer, That the lower or arithmetical notes may want to be excited to vibrate distinctly, by a greater power of harmonic notes than

than what a single string furnishes. There is an observation, in Lord Keeper North's tract on music, which illustrates and confirms my reasoning. He says, p. 20, ' An organ-pipe of a ' very deep base will not speak suddenly, when it is alone; but ' if an octave be in play at the same time, it will answer the quick-' est touch.' I will also observe, that the double base, when played upon alone, gives the most languid tones imaginable; whereas, when accompanied, its tones are firm and vigorous.

CHAP. V.

But I can go one step farther still, and prove, that the arithmetical notes not only may be founded as I have supposed, and in part rendered probable, but that they actually have been founded. It is notorious, that the German horn has the same notes as the trumpet marine, and no other. Now, I remember to have heard Charles, the famous performer on the German horn, found some low notes, which surprised me, and made me suspect that all the theory about that instrument was false. This idea remained with me for many years, and I never could hit upon any solution, till the foregoing theory occurred to me, which seemed to take away all the difficulty. Charles was reckoned an admirable performer, and when he blew the low notes abovementioned, he used no artifice whatever, but what arose from his constant experience and genius. I asked him, at the time, what the notes were which he founded; he told me, but I have now totally forgotten them: these particulars however I remember, which are very much to the purpose, viz. that they were four descending notes, and two of them, as he told me, and as I heard, were what we vulgarly call hemitones; from whence I conclude, that the notes must be G, F, E, E^b; for there are no other low notes but these, that can possibly be founded. If other performers would learn to found them, the use and effect of the horn might be much extended. The close

§ 155. *An illustration on the same subject.*

and

Chap. V. and intimate connection between the arithmetical and harmonic fyftems appears from this, that if you take away F, you deftroy all our mufic at once, but that on the German horn, trumpet marine, and common trumpet; all which inftruments have precifely the fame notes. From the whole, I conclude, that no one has hitherto

> Untwifted all the chains that tie
> The hidden foul of harmony.

But I return to Tartini, who begins his 6th and laft chapter thus:

Chap. VI.

§ 156.

Modern intervals and modulations.

"I am now gotten into a fafe harbor, being returned to the prefent fyftem, relying upon which, I proceed to the examination of thofe particular intervals and modulations, which are commonly ufed in modern mufic, but were not known in the 15th century. If there was any particular compofer who ufed, in thofe times, fuch intervals, of which I am going to treat; or whether the ufe of them began afterwards, I neither know, or is it of importance that I fhould know; it being a fufficient reafon for me, that they are ufed at prefent, to examine their foundation and nature." He then fhews the modern method of managing the fuperfluous 2d, the diminifhed 3d, the diminifhed 4th, the diminifhed 7th, the fuperfluous 6th, and the fuperfluous 5th. But befides the intervals, which he has particularly confidered, other methods are practically deduced from them; but thefe, he fays, are fufficient to give an idea of them. Then adds, "All thefe intervals are included in the prefent univerfal fyftem; they are the very intervals in the mufical example 4, fig. 1, with which the common diatonic fcale is infpiffated, and are chromatic and enharmonic relatively to the prefent fyftem." By thefe laft words he means, that they are not fo relatively to the antient fyftem, of which he profeffed before

fore that he knew nothing. He then shews how these modern
intervals are conformable to his own system; and adds, what is
of great consequence, as follows:

CHAP. VI.

" I grant, that such a kind of music may be practised ac-   § 157.
" cording to the foregoing scale; viz. D, E, F, G✶, A, B♭, C✶, *First bases in*
" D; and with the utmost rigor, according to the foregoing in- *the 3d minor.*
" tervals, both in the harmony of the fundamental base, and
" also in the respective notes of the upper parts. The only rules
" necessary to be observed arise of themselves, from the nature
" of the scale. The first rule is, that none but the notes capable *First rule.*
" of that harmony, from whence the diatonic scale is deduced,
" either can or ought to be first bases; since it is undoubtedly
" true, that every other genus is deduced from the diatonic, as
" its origin and first principle. But this proposition is true to a
" demonstration; because, if the chromatic and enharmonic
" genera arise from the smallest division of the hemitone major,
" you must first suppose the hemitone existing entire. But the
" hemitone is diatonic; therefore the two genera above-mentioned
" cannot exist, unless as founded and established on the diatonic
" genus; therefore much more is the harmony founded upon it.
" In fact, in the notes D, F, G✶, B♭, of example 4, fig. 1,
" the thing is evident. The first interval D, F, is a third minor,
" therefore diatonic, because deduced from the common scale
" D, E, F: Therefore, in the fundamental base, there can be no
" other first bases but D, B♭, A; because, in the above-men-
" tioned scale, there are no other but those assigned."

I must fairly own, that I do not comprehend the latter part of   § 158.
Tartini's reasoning in the foregoing article. I suppose it must *Obscurity of*
be my own fault; for the first bases which he assigns in the system *the last ar-*
ticle.

CHAP. VI. of the 3d minor, are precisely the same which I deduced § 147, in a manner, I imagine, similar to what he hints, when he says, in the preceding article, *that none but notes capable of that harmony,* (i. e. that kind of harmony) *from whence the diatonic scale is deduced, can be first bases.* For the diatonic scale was deduced from the 3ds and 5ths to the prime bases; vide § 53: Therefore e converso, where a 3d and 5th cannot be had to any note, that note cannot be a first base. So much as to his first rule, in relation to what he calls chromatic: In relation to his enharmonic, I need say nothing, having shewed before, article 84, that it is most probably built on a mistake. I proceed now to his second rule.

§ 159.
First bases in the 3d minor.

Second rule.

"There is," says Tartini, "no room left for any supplemental musical accidents; because the second rule ought to be the inalterability of the scale, both in the harmony and in the singing part, otherwise nature itself would be changed; and therefore, if you had a mind to make F first base, in the key of D, taking away ♯ from C, it would be an error. Likewise, if you were to make C natural, G natural, &c. first bases, it would be an error, because it would be an inversion of nature. In fine, as the common scale is unalterable, in relation to the nature of the diatonic genus, so ought this new scale to be unalterable, in relation to the particular genus of the present system; and the more so, because these two scales ought to have certain properties in common. From the same universal principle, the diatonic scale was demonstratively deduced; and the present scale is also deduced demonstratively; therefore both of them are unalterable." I have observed above, § 149, that if you change some of the notes belonging to the scale of the 3d minor, you go into the 3d major almost insensibly; which, I imagine, has occasioned all the confusion in theory relating to

the

the fyftem of the 3d minor; and confequently in the doctrine of practical writers. But to return to Tartini.

CHAP. VI.

" From thefe two rules we may practically treat this kind of
" mufic; (i. e. with a 3d minor) and with an excellent effect, as
" far as my own feeling, and that of other unprejudiced people,
" can determine. See here an example which coft me but little
" ftudy and pains: The tone is transferred out of D, into A,
" for the convenience of the inftruments." This example confifts of a piece in four parts in the 3d minor, where there is not a note which does not belong to that fyftem, and is therefore, I fuppofe, not to be paralleled out of all the immenfe quantity of mufic which has been compofed fince the revival of arts in Europe. As to the chord which Tartini makes ufe of, viz. F, A, C, D✲, which, he fays, contains no difcord, I cannot help being of another opinion. D✲ is no note of the hexachord, and therefore, if my theory is right, it muft be a difcord; but any note belonging to the fcale may be ufed, if it can be refolved properly as D✲ is here upon E. What he fays afterwards, that if you put the harmony thus, D✲, F, A, C, it will be harfh and awkward, is moft likely to be true, becaufe the chord is entirely reverfed. As to what he obferves alfo about the 7th of F, that it ought not to be expreffed by the letter E♭, he is certainly in the right, if E♭ is taken for the 3d minor of C; becaufe there is not the fame interval between E♭, F, in the key of B♭, with a 3d major, as between F, G, in the key of C 3d major, which there ought to be; for from E♭, 3d of C, to F, is a tone minor; whereas from F to G, is a tone major. Tartini thus goes on.

§ 160.

Practical example in the 3d minor.

" I have four things to add in relation to the above-mentioned
" mufical example; the firft is, that I have defignedly difpofed
" the harmony of the four notes, F, A, C, D✲, in different
" manners,

§ 161.

Obfervations on the mufical example.

Chap. VI. " manners, so that the effect, the use and management of
" such intervals might appear. The 2d is, that this particular
" system is capable of many diffonances, without any alteration
" of the given scale, which is easy to observe. The 3d is, that
" though I have called this scale and this system chromatic and
" enharmonic, I do not therefore pretend that it ought to
" be called so, rigoroufly speaking; however, what I shewed in
" the diatonic inspissated scale is certain, viz. that it is analo-
" gous to the chromatic and enharmonic.——But not to give
" myself any trouble about names, it is sufficient for me, that
" the difference of the two scales is obvious, and also of the two
" harmonies; so that the diversity of the system easily appears.
" I am satisfied with having reduced to their genus, nature, and
" principle, those intervals that we sparsedly and indifferently
" use in practise, without rule, and without category. The 4th
" thing to be observed is, and a thing of importance, that the
" four notes, D, F, G*, B♭, which are the foundation of this
" particular system, and which are precisely the diffonances set
" forth in example 4, fig. 1, in relation to the diatonic scale,
" in this system are employed as confonances. Observe therefore,
" on one side, the perfection of their principle, which is the
" circle; and, on the other side, the false idea that musicians
" have hitherto had, that diffonances are intervals disagreeable
" to the ear. I am perfectly sure, that many people will be un-
" commonly pleased with this particular harmony, although
" composed of musical notes that are to all appearance diffonant;
" I am almost certain, that no one will be disgusted with
" them."

§ 162.
Diffonances.

I must observe, upon this occasion, that what Tartini just now said, that the above-mentioned diffonances are treated as confo-nances, is a confirmation of what I maintained above, § 48, that

that there are no diffonances belonging to mufic, but what arife from altering the harmony in fome parts, while in others it remains the fame, &c. This idea is perfectly clear and precife, and, I believe, perfectly true. This far is, I think, at leaft certain, that my author gives no inftance to the contrary, though he has fo fully treated this point. This is an idea I have long had, and am pleafed to fee I have no reafon to alter it. We are now drawing towards a conclufion: But before my author finifhes, he has fomething to offer, that will fully fhew the ufe, and indeed the neceffity, of principles in mufic. It will fhew that ingenuity will not fecure a mufician from wandering out of his way, when he has not a proper guide to direct him. He will be like a pilot, who has neither fun, moon, nor ftars, to look up to. I muft obferve, that the inftances hitherto given by Tartini, of modern intervals and harmonies, are what properly belong to the fyftem of the 3d minor, though by fome looked upon as licenfes; but we are coming to fomething of another nature; for he fays,

CHAP. VI.

"From the particular intervals mentioned above chiefly arife "particular modulations, which many at this time make ufe "of. I fay *chiefly*, becaufe, as will be feen, there may be fome "few modulations not dependant on them. I fay alfo *many*, be- "caufe not every one, who yet knows very well what he is about, "choofes to employ them; nay, I have obferved, that thofe "diftinguifhed artifts, who have exquifite fentiment, joined to "great knowledge in their art, never ufe them at all. Thefe "particular modulations are, in reality, mere artificial deceits; "becaufe, where the modulation ought to pafs, by the nature of "the tone in which the compofition is diftinctly inftituted, to "fuch a determinate and relative tone, it is made by artifice to "pafs to a tone quite diftant, both by nature and relation, from "the principal one firft fettled." He then gives two or three examples,

§ 163.
Extravagant modulations.

CHAP. VI. examples, taken, I suppose, out of the works of composers, and explains whence the artifice, or rather deceit, arises; and observes upon one of those examples, which certainly furnishes a most ingenious way of going wrong, that it is looked upon as a singular beauty and delicacy in the art. It would be in vain to endeavour to give a distinct idea of all these artifices, without musical notes; but it is not on this occasion only that they are wanting; this treatise in many parts points to the original; for my design is not to supersede that excellent work, but to recommend and illustrate it, as far as I am able. He goes on,

§ 164.
Source and use of such modulations.

" I will not take upon me to produce more exquisite instances
" of such modulation; those I have given, which occurred as
" I was writing, are sufficient to give a general idea of them:
" But I take upon me to assign the origin and source of such ar-
" tifices, and deliver my opinion about the use of them." For the reason abovementioned I shall pass over what our author says, about the origin of such musical artifices, arising particularly from notes of double use; and only mention his rule for using them, which cannot be too much inculcated; viz. that they can never have a good effect, but when the harmony does not quit the tone proposed, i. e. the key, which ought to be the principal object. " In a composi-
" tion," says he, " regulated by the tone proposed and establish-
" ed, I am perswaded and convinced, that no other artifices of
" this nature can have place, but those only which do not depart
" from the rigorous modulation belonging to the tone. As to the
" occasions, where all such artifices may be applied in their full
" extent, I am of opinion, that they are to be found in the re-
" citatives of an opera, an oratorio, &c.; because recitatives
" not only are not tied down to a tone proposed and established;
" but, on the contrary, are subservient to the composer, in order
" to dispose and prepare, as he pleases, the tone of the airs or
" songs.

" fongs. Such artifices may fpecifically and precifely produce
" a fine effect, when their force and nature are well underftood,
" and they are adapted to proper words, which will always of-
" fer themfelves in fome part or other of a drama. After all
" that has been faid relating to practife, it remains to be con-
" fidered, whether fuch notes of double ufe can demonftra-
" tively ferve for that purpofe. It is evident in the higheft de-
" gree that they cannot by any means, becaufe the difference be-
" tween the hemitone minor and hemitone major is too great.
" It is true, the fame touch of the harpfichord ferves for
" D^* and E^b, but reafon makes a great difference between
" them; and therefore it is demonftratively impoffible, that the
" two above-mentioned notes may be ufed interchangeably for
" one another. The fame reafon may be applied to all other notes
" of double ufe: therefore, demonftratively, fuch notes cannot
" ferve for fuch a purpofe, for which they are practically made to
" ferve." There may perhaps appear, at firft fight, a contradiction in Tartini, when he fays, that fuch ufe of notes, though
not allowed of by reafon, yet will have a fine effect on certain
occafions: But if we fuppofe him to mean, that fuch notes
cannot be ufed indifferently for one another, but that they may
be ufed, when we do not depart from the harmony of the tone
propofed, as he faid above, the contradiction vanifhes. Here
ends the fixth and laft chapter of the original; and we now
come to what he calls the conclufion, which confifts of fome
obfervations of his own on the foregoing treatife.

CHAP. VI.

I intend to give fome account of this laft part, without entering
into a difcuffion of his principles, which he undertakes to defend
againft fome objections; for neither the objections nor the anfwer to them affect me. After having obferved, that his fyftem
is founded, not on fictions of the mind, but on realities; fuch as
the

CONCLU-
SION.

§ 165.
Want of a practical tract on mufic.

CONCLU-
SION.
the 3d founds, which refult from two or more founds; the founds arifing on the monochord; the founds of confent, which refult from certain given figures of bodies, &c.; he proceeds thus:

"I do not pretend, however, to have made a compleat work, with all poffible particular deductions: For fuch a purpofe, not a fmall tract, but a large volume, would have been neceffary, which you, Sir, diflike as much as I can do. That fuch a volume is wanted, in which the fcience and art of counter-point fhould be contained, and the whole thoroughly compleated, and in a plain manner brought down to the capacity of the common mufical profeffor, I do readily allow; and the man perfectly equal to fuch a tafk lives now amongft us. I fincerely wifh, that, for the benefit of the profeffion, he may be difpofed to undertake it; as all the mufical precepts hitherto publifhed have no foundation but practife only. I cannot ceafe wondering, when I confider how far human fentiment has gone in this affair. It is certain that, many ages ago, men began to compofe; it is certain that, in all thefe ages, there has not appeared one fingle tract, which demonftrates the true principles of harmony, and from them deduces the rules of counterpoint; it is certain alfo, that thefe principles being at laft difcovered, and the principal rules being deduced from them, it appears that practife, by the mere force of genius, has hit upon the principal rules. We muft from hence conclude, that mufic is congenial to us, and that harmony is analogous to human reafon.

§ 166.

Harmony, if unknown, deducible from Tartini's principles.

"Here perhaps you may afk me, Whether, fuppofing there was no fuch thing as mufical harmony known, by vertue alone of this fcience the fame mufical harmony might be deduced, as has been deduced from fentiment? I anfwer, that I think fuch a deduction would be more than poffible. The method
"ufed

CONCLUSION.

" used by me is relative to your commands: You infisted upon
" having a scientifical account of harmony, upon suppofition of
" the exiftence of harmony, and of nothing more; and I am apt
" to believe I have succeeded. For the reft, when you reflect
" on the spirit and substance of this treatife, you will see evi-
" dently the poffibility of such a deduction, independant upon
" sentiment. However, whether it is better to follow sentiment
" rather than science, or the contrary, I do not decide. I con-
" fider, that sentiment is real, and that science is also real: I
" therefore conclude, that it is best to join sentiment to science;
" but I confess sincerely, at the same time, that such a science,
" deduced from such principles, and established in such a man-
" ner, is fitter for a philosopher than a practical musician, and
" therefore full of difficulties for any one. I am perfwaded, that,
" if it comes to be publicly known and cultivated, time, study,
" farther discoveries, and obfervations, will produce a greater
" facility, joined to the greatest utility, in two respects: One is,
" that the human sentiment, supported by real science, and af-
" fisted by physical truths, that are inseparable from it, would
" be better explained, and rendered more extensive; from thence
" we might derive hopes of arriving, by another road, to that
" point which the antients arrived at. The other advantage is,
" that a discovery might be made, one of these days, what and
" how great the extent of physico-harmonic science is, of which
" music is but a small part. Many learned and profound scho-
" lars have interested themselves in music, confidered in that
" point of light, and which they looked upon as the true one;
" and in confequence have advanced and deduced things true,
" wonderful, and worthy of the highest praise. When it comes
" to be looked upon in this new light, which in relation to har-
" mony, I am convinced, is the only true and legitimate one;
" and men of learning will deign to intereft themselves again;
" they

CONCLU- "they would know, much better than I can do, that things of
SION.   "more weight, I may say, of the greatest importance, are con-
         "tained in it. But this does not appertain to me, who am only
         "interested to serve you in your particular inclination.

§ 167.

Rules deduci- "I return therefore to my business; and affirm, that when
ble from Tar- "you have examined, in your own rigorous method, the sub-
tini's princi- "stantial parts of the system, and find that it stands the trial per-
ples.   "fectly, you will make your own particular deductions; and I
             "am certain that you will form such as are just and true; and
             "that nothing will escape your consideration. If I say, for
             "example, that the rule which forbids us to use two successive
             "octaves, and two successive 5ths, between the parts of the
             "harmony, derives its principle not only in general from the
             "two systems, harmonic and arithmetical, in which the succes-
             "sive ratios are always different; but specifically from the duple
             "and sesquialter, as fundamental ratios of the harmonic system;
             "and therefore, on account of their dignity and significancy, en-
             "tirely distinct from other ratios: If I say, that the rule of con-
             "trary motions between the parts has its foundation in the mu-
             "sical example, fig. 1, example 3; in which not only the con-
             "trary motion, when compared with example 2, is evident;
             "but there is moreover the indication of the law of such pro-
             "gression from note to note, which, by degrees, or by jumps,
             "are allowed between the parts and the base: If I say, the law
             "for forming real subjects (a distinct artifice, and the source of
             "many others) arises substantially from the harmonic and arith-
             "metical division of the octave; and therefore the octave being
             "divided harmonically thus, C G C, if C G is proposed, G C
             "ought to follow; and so, if the octave being divided arithme-
             "tically thus, C F C, if C F is proposed, F C ought to follow:
             "If I say either this or any other thing, by way of occasional
                                                               "example,

"example, I am sensible I say nothing but what is merely su- CONCLU-
"perfluous for you. I repeat, therefore, that if you, illustrious SION.
"Sir, find the present system true, you will have, considering
"your sagacity and profoundness, an opportunity of making
"deductions for many years to come; and I have reason to be-
"lieve, that, you being young, and I old, you will go on making
"deductions when I shall no longer be in the land of the living.
"Whatever happens, as long as I do live, I shall live devoted
"to you, from duty, respect, and inclination; and therefore
"always disposed to obey your commands, as I have done on
"this occasion." Thus ends Tartini's treatise on music; but
I cannot quit the subject without adding a few selected observations, which I could not introduce into the body of the
work, without interrupting the main business too much; some,
perhaps, will think I have done so already: but, however
that may be, here follows the Appendix; after saying of my
great guide and constant instructor, what Petavius said of Scaliger,
whom he had criticised with great severity,

DUM ERRAT DOCET.

APPENDIX.

§ 168.
Ægyptian music.

I SAID, § 54, that the art of mufic was undoubtedly firft begun in Ægypt, and from thence propagated over the reft of the world, wherever any true mufic has been known. This affertion, I am fenfible, will feem very fingular, and perhaps rafh, to thofe who remember what Diodorus Siculus, lib. i, fays, viz. ' that
' it was not the cuftom, amongft the Ægyptians, to learn mufic;
' for that they looked upon it not only as ufelefs, but noxious,
' being perfuaded that it rendered the minds of men effeminate.'
This paffage of Diodorus has had fuch weight with all the writers on mufic, whom I have had an opportunity of confulting, that they feem to have been convinced, that the Ægyptians did not apply themfelves to mufic. Yet, if we may give credit to a much better authority, as to every thing that relates to Ægypt, this opinion is without foundation. Plato, who travelled into that country, with a view of getting acquainted with the arts and fciences that flourifhed there, tells us quite another ftory. Now we cannot fuppofe him to have been negligent in getting information about an art of which he was particularly fond, as is known to every one who has looked into his writings. Let us hear then what he fays on this fubject.

§ 169.
An account of Ægyptian mufic, out of Plato.

' Athen. The plan which we have been laying down for the edu-
' cation of youth, was known long ago to the Ægyptians, viz. that
' nothing but beautiful forms and fine mufic fhould be permitted
' to enter into the affemblies of young people. Having fettled
what

'what those forms and music should be, they exhibited them
'in their temples; nor was it allowable for painters, or other
'imitative artists, to innovate or invent any forms different from
'what were established; nor is it now lawful, either in painting,
'statuary, or any of the branches of music, to make any altera-
'tion. Upon examining, therefore, you will find, that the
'pictures and statues made 10,000 years ago, are not only not
'10,000 times, but not a jot, better or worse, than what they
'make now. Clin. What you say is wonderful. Athen. Yes;
'It is in the true spirit of legislation and policy. Other things
'practised amongst that people may, perhaps, be blameable;
'but what they ordained about music is right; and it deserves
'consideration, that they were able to make laws about things
'of this kind, firmly establishing such melody as was fitted to
'rectify the perverseness of nature. This must have been the
'work of the Deity, or of some divine man; as, in fact, they
'say in Ægypt, that the music which has been so long preserved,
'was composed by Isis, and the poetry likewise.' Plat. p. 789.
This testimony of Plato contains a full answer to Diodorus; for
it appears, that the Ægyptians were so far from neglecting music, that they laid the greatest stress upon it. The only question
then is, how far they carried that art, which shall be the next
consideration.

It is universally agreed, that the Hermes of the Greeks was §. 170.
the Thoth of the Ægyptians; and therefore I shall produce no Hermes in-
proofs of the truth of this opinion. That the Græcian Hermes *vented the*
invented the seven-stringed lyre is also generally believed; vide *heptachord.*
Hom. hymn in Merc. v. 51; Lucian Dialog. Apoll. et Vulc.;
Schol. in Arat. artic. Χελυς.—Nicom. Man. lib. ii, says thus:
'It is related, that Mercury invented the lyre, which he made
'of a tortoise, and having put seven strings to it, gave it to Or-
'pheus

APPENDIX. ' pheus, and taught him how to ufe it. Orpheus taught Tha-
' myris and Linus to play upon it; and Linus taught Hercules,
' by whom he [Linus] was killed. Orpheus alfo taught Am-
' phion, who built Thebes, with feven gates, to the founds of
' his feven ftrings. When Orpheus was killed by the Thracian
' women, it is faid, his lyre was thrown into the fea, and car-
' ried to Antiffa, a city of Lefbos, and that fome fifhermen hap-
' pening to meet with it, gave it to Terpander; who, having
' adorned it very finely, took it with him into Ægypt, and
' fhewed it to the priefts there, and gave himfelf out as the in-
' ventor.' I chofe to give this account at length, as it exhibits
a ftriking fpecimen of the genius of the Greeks, who had full as
much vanity as ingenuity; which is faying a great deal of both.
In fpite therefore of this ridiculous claim, we muft allow the
Ægyptians to have been the inventors of the heptachord; and
if this was the cafe, nothing more is neceffary to make good my
affertion, that the art of mufic was begun in Ægypt, &c.: For,
as furely as the Greeks learned it of the Ægyptians, fo furely did
the Romans learn it of the Greeks, and the reft of the world of
the Romans.

§ 171.   But it will be objected, that the mufic propagated over Europe
Probably the has not been that confifting of feven ftrings only, which is Ægyp-
octachord alfo. tian; but that confifting of eight, or more, which is Græcian, as
being invented by Pythagoras. To this objection I anfwer, that I
mentioned, § 13, fome fufpicions why I think his claim not
quite clear: Amongft the reft, I cited a paffage out of Plutarch,
about the divifion of the feafons of the year, which plainly alludes
to the numbers of the octave. This divifion is faid, by Arift.
Quint. p. 145, to have been the invention of Pythagoras; but
he is certainly miftaken; for making fpring as 6, autumn as 8,
winter as 9, fummer as 12, we fhall have 62, 83, 93, 125
days.

days nearly for thofe feafons refpectively; which may probably be right for Ægypt or Chaldæa, but certainly not for Greece; where, according to Euripides, and the concurrent teftimony of the old writers, fpring and autumn confifts each of 60, winter and fummer each of 120 days nearly. But Pythagoras, who was, if not 22 years, as Iamblichus fays, yet certainly a long time, amongft the Ægyptians, and being initiated in their myfteries, was better acquainted with their learning than any other foreigner whatever, in all probability firft taught his countrymen the octave expreffed by 6, 8, 9, 12; and from thence the very invention of it was attributed to him. However, to fupport my affertion, it is not neceffary to fuppofe the Ægyptians to have invented the two disjunct tetrachords. We may have a great variety of very fine mufic with feven notes only; at leaft the Greeks thought fo; for no more notes were ufed in the Dorian, Phrygian, and Lydian modes practifed by Anacreon; vide Athenæum, p. 635; and Pindar mentions his lyre as having only feven ftrings, Pyth. 2, 130, et Nem. 5, 43: Yet both thefe poets, who were nearly of the fame age, lived after the fuppofed difcovery of Pythagoras; and Pindar, particularly, wrote the fecond Pythian ode above 60 years after that philofopher was famous. So much for my affertion, § 54.

APPENDIX.

I will take this opportunity of obferving, that the advantage arifing from the octachord of Pythagoras confifted in this, that whereas in the heptachord, where two tetrachords were joined together without an intermediate tone, you could not add another fimilar tetrachord, without going out of the key; in the octachord, on the contrary, you may add as many fimilar tetrachords as you pleafe, and ftill keep in the fame key. This will become evident by confidering fig. 10; where B, C, D, E; E, F, G, A, are two fimilar conjunct tetrachords; for from B to C

§ 172. *Advantages of the octachord.*

APPENDIX. is a hemitone, and from E to F is also a hemitone; from C to D, as from F to G, is a tone, &c.; and the key is C. Add now another similar conjunct tetrachord, viz. A, B, C, D, and it is clear that B must be lowered, in order to get the hemitone required; and thus the key is altered; for we are now got into F. B, thus lowered, is called B fa, and the scale, scala mollis; as the other in C is called scala dura; but they are both in the 3d major.

§ 173.
Ægyptian sculpture and painting.

Norden.

We have no method left of getting any idea of the old Ægyptian music, but by supposing (what I believe is always the case, and to the disgrace of conceited ignorance has hitherto proved to be so) a proportional degree of perfection in arts of a similar nature, as music, painting, and sculpture, may truly be said to be. If this supposition may be allowed, there are remains in Ægypt of the two last-mentioned arts, sufficient to enable us to form a judgment of their music; and such remains as will furnish us with a very favourable idea of it. Many testimonies might be produced on this occasion; but I shall confine myself to two only, who, from their known character, are fully adequate to my purpose. Norden, Voiage en Egypte, p. 102, mentions ' obelisks
' adorned with hieroglyphics, that one beholds with admiration;'
p. 170, speaking of some hieroglyphics, ' agreeable,' says he,
' to behold at a distance; and when one is near, the colours
' have a charming effect:' Again, ibid. ' It is surprising to see
' how the gold, the ultramarine, and other colours, have pre-
' served their brilliancy to this time. Perhaps I shall be asked,
' How all these lively colours could be so blended together? I
' own, I cannot tell.' Again, p. 173, ' A colossal head, dressed
' in the antient Ægyptian taste, finished with a great deal of art
' and patience, with a simplicity that is charming; which makes
' me believe it came from the hands of a great master.'

M. 1

M. le Comte de Caylus, Antiquités Ægyptiennes, &c. Vol. I, APPENDIX. p. 4, says, 'It muſt be owned, the Ægyptian ſculptors felt and expreſſed grandeur; and it is in this that the chief and moſt eſ- ſential part of their art conſiſts; becauſe this alone raiſes the mind of the ſpectator.' Such a teſtimony, from ſuch a judge, is a ſufficient anſwer to any objections about the excellence of the Ægyptian taſte in the fine arts; and I might leave every un-prejudiced reader to draw his concluſions. But there is another paſſage in Caylus, which I cannot omit producing on this occa-ſion, as it confirms what I cited out of Plato, § 169; and as the paſſage in Plato ſolves a difficulty which Caylus ſeems at a loſs how to account for: 'Arts,' ſays he, 'being progreſſive in all other countries, we cannot but ſuppoſe that they were ſo amongſt the Ægyptians; yet their works, ſo far from favouring ſo na-tural a preſumption, have always offered me hitherto an equality of taſte, form, and workmanſhip, which ſurpriſed me. I ima-gined, therefore, that I ought to attribute this uniformity to a prodigious antiquity, which hindered their firſt works from coming down to us. I imagined, afterwards, that the propor-tions being once known and admitted, ſuperſtition and ſcruple had laid an obſtacle in the way of that ſucceſſive progreſs, to which nature and practiſe lead, in a country eſpecially, which, knowing nothing in general but its own productions, was an-tiently deprived of the aſſiſtance that ariſes from compariſon. With this idea, which was formed upon objects that I had under my eye, I have more than once mentioned with an elogium the equality of proportions obſerved by the Ægyptians.' He then gives an account of a figure of the higheſt antiquity, without beauty or proportion; and this he takes for a proof, that art had, in Ægypt as well as in other countries, its progreſs towards per-fection. No doubt it had: But that degree of perfection, which

§ 174.

Egyptian sculpture.

of Caylus.

ſatisfied

APPENDIX. satisfied the Ægyptians, had long been obtained, though not 10,000, yet perhaps above 2000 years, before the time of Plato; and this passage out of Caylus confirms Plato's account.

§ 175.
Greek music, its effect.

Tartini barely mentions, vide § 91, the names of Plato and Aristotle, as vouchers and witnesses of the effect of antient music on the passions. I intend to go farther, and not only give some account of what these two philosophers say, but also to add the testimony of other grave and credible witnesses; in order to confirm what has been doubted of, even by men who had no prejudices against music in general, or that of the Greeks in particular. But that what I shall have to say on this subject may have its proper weight, in relation to the merit of the antient music, it will be necessary first to remove some difficulties, started by one of great authority; I mean, that most acute mathematician Dr. Wallis; who, I suppose, knew more of the antient music than any modern, except Meibomius. The former, in Philosophical Transactions abridged by Lowthorp, Vol. I. p. 618, says thus: 'I take it for granted, that much of the reports concerning the 'great effects of music in former times, beyond what is to be 'found in latter ages, is highly hyberbolical, and next to fabu- 'lous; and therefore great abatements, &c.' This first article is merely taken for granted, and prefatory. The second article gives for reason ' that music (to any tolerable degree) was then, ' (if not a new, at least) a rare thing; which the rustics, on ' whom it is reported to have had such effects, had never heard ' before; and on such, a little music will do great feats; as ' we find at this day a fiddle or a bagpipe at a country morrice- ' dance.'

§ 176.
Greek music vindicated.

To speak freely on this occasion, I cannot help being amazed to find so crude an opinion delivered by a man of Dr. Wallis's character,

character, on a subject, which, as appears by his excellent edition of Ptolemy, employed his thoughts very much. Had he confined this unfavourable judgment of the antient Greek music to some fabulous accounts which we meet with here and there, about its effect on various kinds of animals; as, wolves, elephants, mares, wild boars, deer, dolphins, &c. it would hardly have been worth while to contradict him; though some of those stories are most undoubtedly founded on truth; because they do not so much prove the excellence of the musician, as the exquisite workmanship of the great Author of nature. Had Dr. Wallis's censure gone no farther than this, I should have said nothing about it; but when I consider that it throws a suspicion on the testimony of the greatest men of antiquity, I cannot but think it deserves some examination. When I say the greatest men, I mean such as had the highest reputation in the most enlightened times of Greece, i. e, the most enlightened times that the annals of the world mention. I shall not at present cite the opinion of those great men about the effect of music. This I shall mention afterwards. I shall now only consider in a general way what probably must have been the state of music in the time of Plato and Aristotle, who are the chief authors that give such incredible accounts of its effects.

APPENDIX.

§ 177. *Music not rare in the time of Homer.*

Homer lived above 400 years before the philosophers above-mentioned, according to the account which brings them the nearest together. Does it then appear that music, even in his days, was a rare thing? So far from it that we have an account of music in various ways, perpetually occurring in his poems, particularly in the Odyssey, which has been justly called Κατοπ'ρον τȣ ἐιȣ ανθρωπινȣ; and which we may therefore suppose to give a true picture of what he daily saw before his eyes. In the Iliad and Odyssey together there are above fifty places where music is mentioned;

APPENDIX. tioned; in some of which the tibia and cithara are employed—In some singing and playing on instruments are called the companions and ornaments of a feast—In others responsive choral singing at a funeral is described—In others singing to the cithara to cheer the labourers at a vintage—In others, Apollo preludes, and the Muses sing alternately—In others, Phemius or Demodocus performs a kind of musical drama; or what ought rather perhaps to be called a cantata, with a regular subject: from whence I conclude that the music must at least have been tolerable; for we cannot suppose that Homer would have thought it worth while to celebrate even good poetry, accompanied with such wretched music as a bagpipe can produce. Nay, we cannot, without being extravagant, suppose that barbarism and civility could be so absurdly coupled together, whatever seeming proofs, either antient or modern, may have been produced to the contrary.

§ 178.
Nor after him. After Homer some of the first writers were the Lyric and Dithyrambic poets, as the two Alcmans, Simonides the elder, Terpander, Arion, Stesichorus, Sappho, &c. and these were of course practical musicians and composers; and we must necessarily suppose that music was rather improved than the contrary, under such masters. Next came the theatrical poets, and they too set their own pieces to music; and that the Greek tragedy was throughout set to music, appears by a passage in Aristotle, which is the only testimony I shall quote in proof of my assertion: ' The Hypodorian and Hypophry-
' gian modes are improper for the chorus, but more suitable
' for the scenic personages.' Vol. 2. 770. problem. I may perhaps have occasion to mention Aristotle's reasons for this opinion afterwards.

But

But again, mufic was fo far from being *rare* at the time when the authors lived who give an account of its wonderful effects, that it was a regular part of education. This is fo well known a fact, that to undertake to prove it would be a mere oftentation of reading. Every fchool-boy knows what Cornelius Nepos fays of Epaminondas; and the ftory of Themiftocles related by Cicero, is almoft as well known. Inftead therefore of citing fuch trite inftances, and fifty others fimilar to them, I will give one from amongft a people who are frequently reprefented as rather averfe to the ftudy of mufic. Xenophon, p. 661. fays, that Agefilaus at the folemn feftival, called Hyacinthia, performed his part in the Pæan fung to Apollo, being appointed thereto by the mafter of the chorus. From hence it appears that mufic muft have made a part of education amongft the Lacedemonians, otherwife we cannot fuppofe that one of their kings could, with any decency, have been appointed to fing on a public occafion. This ftory would afford many reflections; but I have no room left to wander into all the paths where my copious fubject would lead me.

Appendix.

§ 179. *Mufic not rare in Greece.*

What fhall we fay to the paffage cited by Athenæus out of Ariftoxenus, p. 632.? 'I and a few others, recollecting what
' mufic once was, and confidering what it now is, as corrupted
' by the theatre, act like the people of Pofidonium, who annually
' celebrate a feftival after the Greek manner, in order to keep up
' the memory of what they once were; and before they depart,
' with tears deplore the barbarous ftate they are brought into by
' the Tufcans or Romans.' Is not this paffage a convincing proof that mufic muft have been carried to a great degree of perfection as early as the time of Plato and Ariftotle? What fhall we fay about the care of the Greek muficians in adjufting the modes, inftruments, and rhythm together; and this with a fcrupulous ex-actitude,

§ 180. *Mufic corrupted in the time of Ariftoxenus.*

APPENDIX. aptitude, that favors to us of whim and affectation. Instances of this sort abound in the ancient writers. Is it usual for arts that are little understood, and only practised amongst rustics, to be so very nice? What shall we say to the custom amongst the Athenians of erecting monuments with tripods in honor of the tribe which gained the prize in a chorus, where the names of the furnisher and teacher, the number of performers, and whether men or boys, were recorded? Was music rare when a whole people contended thus with one another by bodies, which of them could produce the ablest musicians? Or can we suppose the music to be ordinary, or even indifferent, when it was studied by so many ingenious rivals? Let any one consider all these circumstances, and decide whether it is possible to reconcile them with Dr. Wallis's opinion; who, after having observed that music with the ancients took in poetry, dancing, gesture, as well as singing and playing; says thus: 'Now all this together must needs operate strongly on 'the fancies and affections of ordinary people, unacquainted with 'such kind of treatments.'

§ 181. 'But,' says Dr. Wallis, 'the antients had not consorts of two, *Antients had* 'three, four, or more parts or voices.' Maibomius asserts much *music in parts.* the same thing; and this is, one may almost say, the universal opinion. Some, however, of the writers on music have produced passages out of the antients, which seem to imply the contrary; but which are not looked upon as conclusive by others: Such as that out of Seneca, Epist. 84: 'Non vides quam multorum vo- 'cibus,' &c. mentioned by If. Vossius de Poemat. Cant. &c. p. 82; where perhaps nothing but octaves are implied. Another passage cited by him, out of the piece de Mundo, attributed to Aristotle, seems to be more to the purpose $μουσικη$ $οξεις$, &c. i. e. music, mixing together acute and grave, long and short sounds, forms one harmony out of different voices. Wallis also has produced.

duced a paſſage out of Ptolemy, which he thinks may infer muſic in parts. Ptol. Harm. p. 317. But the ſtrongeſt paſſage which I have met with, in relation to this long-diſputed point, is in Plato; a paſſage which I have never ſeen quoted, and which I ſhall tranſlate : ' Young men ſhould be taught to ſing to the lyre,
' on account of the clearneſs and preciſion of the ſounds, ſo that
' they may learn to render tone for tone. But to make uſe of
' different ſimultaneous notes, and all the variety belonging to
' the lyre, this ſounding one kind of melody and the poet ano-
' ther—to mix a few notes with many, ſwift with ſlow, grave
' with acute, conſonant with diſſonant, &c. muſt not be thought
' of; as the time allotted for this part of education is too ſhort
' for ſuch a work." Plat. 895. I am ſenſible, that objections may be made to ſome parts of this tranſlation, as of the words πυκνοτης, μανοτης, and ανιςφωνοις; but I have not deſignedly diſ-guiſed what I took to be the true ſenſe of them, after due conſideration. It appears then, upon the whole, that the antients were acquainted with muſic in parts, but did not generally make uſe of it.

APPENDIX.

But Dr. Wallis enters into particulars, and objects to the ſto-ries about Orpheus, Amphion, Timotheus, &c. Now, what is ſaid about the two firſt of theſe muſicians, is ſo plainly poetical, that a child cannot miſtake it; and perhaps may only mean, that men were incited and encouraged to work by the power of their muſic ; as Nicomachus indeed ſeems to ſay nothing more, in the paſſage about Amphion cited § 170 ; and as the Argonauts are ſaid, by Apollonius Rhodius, to have been incited to row by the lyre of Orpheus. This kind of encouragement was not unuſual amongſt the antients. Homer mentions a boy ſinging, and playing on the cithara, to the labourers at the vintage ; and Euripides, a muſician, playing on the pipe to the rowers; Iphig. in Taur. v. 1125. This, I ſay, might poſſibly be the whole that

§ 182. *Stories about Orpheus.*

was

APPENDIX. was meant by the stories about Orpheus and Amphion. But we are not obliged to confine ourselves to that meaning, as we have sufficient reason to believe that their music was uncommonly touching, and capable of producing any effect almost within the limits of possibility. The reason we have for thinking thus highly of their music, is not drawn from theory, which is a most deceitful guide in cases of this kind; though the only one which Dr. Wallis had or could have to follow. No, we stand upon other, and better ground, and such as may be firmly relied upon; I mean the testimony of some who heard, if not the music of Orpheus and Amphion, yet that of musicians full as old.

§ 183.
Music of Olympus.

Plato, speaking of the music which remained in his time, of Marsyas and his disciple Olympus, says, p. 567, ' that it was most divine, and adapted in a very particular manner to stir and affect the mind.' This testimony of Plato, who was himself a practical musician, and lived at a time when music flourished in an eminent degree, ought to have great weight. Again, Aristotle says, p. 455. that the compositions of Olympus raised an enthusiasm in the soul. Lastly, the music of Olympus was preserved to the days of Plutarch, who says, it surpassed any music then known. Now, Olympus was at least as old as Orpheus; and it was he who composed the *curule* song, Plutarch, p. 1133, which caused Alexander to catch up his arms, while Antigenidas was performing it; Id. p. 335. As to the effect of the recent music in the time of Plato and Aristotle, they both speak of it in very strong terms. Plato, after mentioning, p. 906. several of the modes then in use, excludes some, and admits others into his republic, on account of their different effects on the morals; and Aristotle says, p. 770. vol. 2. that the Subphrygian mode affects the mind with something like madness, and drives it into a kind of Bacchanalian state. ibid. p. 455.

455. That the Phrygian mode raises enthusiasm. 'This,' adds he, 'is rightly affirmed by those who are conversant in things of this kind; for they speak from what they see actually happen.' It appears then that the two above-mentioned philosophers perfectly agree in their opinion about the power of music, and the propriety of making it a part of education; though the disciple takes every occasion to contradict his master, especially in relation to his republic. It is curious to observe the different motives they make use of to recommend music. Plato, who was given up to the sublime of speculation, says, that music accustoms the mind to order, and thereby allures it to the love of vertu; which is nothing but moral order; and so raises it gradually to the contemplation and love of that being, who alone is the source of all order, both natural and moral. This was the way of reasoning of that great philosopher; and the same way of reasoning made him recommend the study of astronomy, and of the sciences subservient to it, as arithmetic and geometry. He thought, all other views but that, beneath the dignity of man. His disciple, Aristotle, talks more like a man of the world on this occasion, as he does in all other parts of his philosophy; and says, we should not only be taught to do business with honor, but also, to be idle with dignity;—that it is unworthy of a gentleman to make profit the only view in all pursuits;—that it is scarcely possible to judge rightly, in any art which we have not practised; and therefore, in order to qualify people to be pleased with nothing but what is fine in music, they must practise it in their youth;—that, as young folks can never be at rest, their parents ought to provide them with some innocent amusement; as Archytas contrived a rattle for children, in order to keep them from doing mischief.

§ 184.

But to return to my main purpose, which was to shew, that the stories mentioned, about the effect of the antient music, were not

APPENDIX.

The power of antient music proved from testimony.

APPENDIX. not owing either to its scarcity, or the rusticity of the audience. This point, I imagine, must appear very evident to any impartial reader, by what I have already said ; but, if it were necessary, I could with the greatest ease produce the testimony of poets, historians, soldiers, statesmen, lawyers, divines, philosophers, of the highest character for wisdom and gravity, living in several ages and countries, all concurring to confirm the opinion of Plato and Aristotle; and, what is extraordinary, I do not remember that Lucian, who takes every opportunity of exposing the philosophers, ever once ridicules them for it. If all these circumstances are not sufficient to gain our belief, merely because we moderns have not the same musical power; then have the Kamschatcans a right to decide, that it is impossible to foretell an eclipse ; or to represent all the elements of speech, by about twenty-four marks.

§ 185.
Lacedæmonian *senatus-consultum.*

Though I think it unnecessary to produce the opinion of any other private person on this subject after those I have already mentioned; yet it may not be amiss to produce the judgment of a nation ; and I the rather produce it, because, besides the weight it must carry, it contains a curious piece of antiquity. The piece I mean is a senatus-consultum of the Lacedæmonians preserved in Boethius ; and is as follows: WHEREAS TIMOTHEUS, THE MILESIAN, COMING TO OUR CITY, HAS DEFORMED THE ANTIENT MUSIC; AND LAYING ASIDE THE USE OF THE SEVEN-STRINGED LYRE, AND INTRODUCING A MULTIPLICITY OF NOTES, ENDEAVOURS TO CORRUPT THE EARS OF OUR YOUTH BY MEANS OF THESE HIS NOVEL AND COMPLICATED CONCEITS, WHICH HE CALLS CHROMATIC; BY HIM EMPLOYED IN THE ROOM OF OUR ESTABLISHED, ORDERLY, AND SIMPLE MUSIC; AND WHEREAS, &C. IT THEREFORE SEEMETH GOOD TO US THE KING AND EPHORI, AFTER HAVING CUT OFF THE SUPERFLUOUS STRINGS OF HIS LYRE, AND LEAVING ONLY SEVEN THEREON, TO BANISH

THE

THE SAID TIMOTHEUS OUT OF OUR DOMINIONS, THAT EVERY ONE APPENDIX.
BEHOLDING THE WHOLESOME SEVERITY OF THIS CITY MAY BE DE-
TERRED FROM BRINGING IN AMONGST US ANY UNBECOMING CUS-
TOMS, &c.

§ 186. *Observations on the Senatus-consultum.*

I have not produced the whole, nor do I pretend to have given a literal tranſlation of this remarkable ſenatus-conſultum, which has been very much corrupted by tranſcribers. I have taken the ſenſe of it as corrected by Iſ. Caſaubon in his notes on Athenæus. The corrections are highly probable, but not ſufficient to furniſh throughout a grammatical conſtruction; for which reaſon I aimed at nothing farther than the general ſenſe, which I muſt obſerve for the ſatisfaction of the Engliſh reader is clear enough, even without Caſaubon's corrections. I muſt farther obſerve upon this occaſion, that this is the very Timotheus who is ſaid by ſome to have produced ſuch an effect on Alexander by his muſic—that this was the third time that the Lacedæmonians had in much the ſame way put a ſtop to any innovation in muſic, as thinking it of the greateſt conſequence to the ſtate. Plutarch. Inſtitut. Lacon. p. 239. vol. 2. et id. p. 799. vol 1. That only ſeven ſtrings were uſed long after the octachord was ſettled by Pythagoras; vide § 171—that the chromatic was looked upon as unbecoming a grave and manly people, vide § 150.—And laſtly, that it appears that the very two nations who are ſuppoſed to have paid very little regard to muſic, viz. the Ægyptians and Lacedæmonians, in fact are found to have laid the greateſt ſtreſs upon it, by making it in ſo particular a manner the object of national concern. Vide § 169.

§ 187. *The power of muſic proved from theory.*

Having ſaid all that I think neceſſary, in point of teſtimony, upon this ſubject, I ſhall now come to theory, and conſider, whether that may not tend to prove the ſame thing. Cicero.

T   Tuſc.

APPENDIX. Tusc. 1, says, that Aristoxenus thought the soul was nothing but a certain tuning of the body, as in the voice and on the lyre, which is called harmony; so that, from the nature and figure of the body, various motions are produced, as sounds are in singing. To this it is answered, that he was so fond of his darling music, that he wanted to transfer every thing to that art; and that we can understand what harmony means from the intervals of sounds; but how the figure of the body, without a soul, can produce harmony, does not appear. As the works of Aristoxenus, where this doctrine was contained, are lost, it is not possible to know whether or not his sense be truly represented. Several of the antient philosophers, especially of the Pythagorean and Platonic sects, supposed the soul to be made according to harmony. This notion was misrepresented by some, as if they had said the soul was nothing but harmony. Both Plutarch and Proclus take notice of this misrepresentation in relation to Plato. By soul was frequently meant amongst the antients, not the rational principle in man, which is capable of perceiving universal truths, but a subtile kind of matter spread over the grosser body. This kind of matter man was supposed to have in common with the brutes; it was looked upon, either as itself of a sensitive nature, or peculiarly adapted to convey the notices of things to the immaterial presiding mind. This way of considering the material soul is well illustrated by the Stoics, who supposed it to consist of eight parts; viz. the 5 senses, the 6th the vocal, the 7th the spermatic, and the 8th the governing or intellectual part; from which last all the other parts are spread through their proper organs like the arms of the cuttle-fish. Plutar. p. 898, vol. 2.

§ 188. Aristides Quint. de musicâ, p. 106. exhibits a doctrine something resembling that of the Stoics just mentioned; for he talks of the meninges and nervous membranes, like the spider's web, but hollow;

Nervous system.

hollow; containing a spirit within them; by which membranes the soul, and not the body, is put in motion. How far anatomy had been advanced in the time of Ariſtides, who was contemporary with Trajan, I cannot ſay; but the paſſage above-cited ſeems to ſuppoſe ſome knowledge of the nervous ſyſtem, which is univerſally allowed at preſent to be an expanſion of the brain, from the meninges over all the body. It is alſo univerſally agreed, that the nerves are the organs of ſenſe and motion, but in what manner is diſputed. Baglivi, who was one of the firſt conſiderable writers on this ſubject, once thought that theſe phænomena aroſe from animal ſpirits which paſs through the nerves. Afterwards he changed his mind, and attributed every thing to oſcillation. But to ſtick to the auditory nerves, which at preſent is my only concern, Valſalva, who had made a particular ſtudy of the ear, accounts for the effect of ſounds by the vibrations of the nerves, and compares the nerves to muſical ſtrings. Vide de Aur. humanâ, cap. 6.

_{APPENDIX.}

This theory, however natural it may ſeem at firſt ſight, has been laid aſide by later writers. Haller in his lineæ phyſiologicæ, urges, that the nerves cannot vibrate unleſs they are hard, unleſs they are ſtretched, and unleſs they are fixed. But nothing in them appears of this ſort. Beſides, nerves when cut do not contract; and ſome of them are faſtened down, as thoſe of the heart to the arteries, p. 193. Haller therefore recurs to the old ſyſtem of animal ſpirits, which ſurely is a very unphiloſophical idea, conſidered in any light whatever; for no man will pretend to ſay what theſe ſpirits are—whether any ſpirits paſſing through the nerves do at all exiſt—or whether any ſpirits whatever can anſwer the purpoſes for which they are invented. On the other hand if it is poſſible for a nerve to be put into motion throughout its whole length, by means of ſome impreſſion at either extremity, then every difficulty vaniſhes, in relation to that ſyſtem which

§ 189.

Animal ſpirits.

ſeems

APPENDIX. ſeems ſo natural; and theſe ſpirits may be remanded back to their native region, where they will be more properly employed to 'tread the ooze of the ſalt deep—to run upon the ſharp wind of 'the north—and to do buſineſs in the veins of the earth—when 'it is baked with froſt;' than to carry intelligence backward and forward between the brain, and the other parts of the body. Let us then ſee what probable ſolution may be found.

§ 190.   But before I enter upon this ſubject, I muſt obſerve that
Vibrations not Haller's objections relate only to vibrations, ſuch as are produced
neceſſary for on a muſical ſtring; and not to all kinds of continued motions
muſic. whatever. The whole buſineſs therefore is, to find ſome motion in the nerves that is perfectly regular, may be propagated from end to end, and is not liable to the defects mentioned above. If this can be done, one may have as clear a conception how the ſoul receives intelligence by means of the nerves, as how a ſpider ſituated in the midſt of its web, may be made ſenſible of the ſlighteſt impreſſion made on any part of its delicate texture.

§ 191.   But to come to what I take to be a ſolution of the foregoing
Harmonic un- difficulties mentioned by Haller. Galileo in his Diſcorſi e Dimoſ-
dulations. trat. Mathem. toward the end of the firſt dialogue, has the following paſſage. 'We plainly ſee the circulation of the medium about 'the reſounding body to diffuſe to a large ſpace, by making a 'drinking glaſs to ſound, that has ſome water in it, by rubbing the 'rim or edge of it with the tip of one's finger; for we ſhall thus 'ſee the water in the glaſs to undulate in a moſt regular order; 'which effect will yet be more clearly ſeen if we put the foot of 'the glaſs in the bottom of a veſſel of reaſonable bigneſs, and fill 'it with water nearly to the glaſs's rim, and then make it ſound by 'rubbing it round as before, with the tip of one's finger: for 'then we ſhall ſee the circulations in the water to be moſt regular,

and

' and with great velocity to spread to a great distance round about
' the glass: Nay, I have often happened to see, in making a
' pretty big glass almost full of water to sound as before, the
' waves formed with an exact equality: but the tone of the glass
' happening sometimes to rise an eight higher; I have seen at that
' very instant every one of the said waves to divide themselves
' into two: which accident most plainly proves the form of the
' octave to be double.' From this phænomena it follows that
harmonic undulations may take place where vibrations cannot;
and I think what we see happen in animals of the serpent kind
will help to explain how the nerves may be affected. When
animals of that kind move in their natural way, you see regular
undulations throughout their body. Thus Milton, speaking of
the serpent, B. ix. v. 496, ' Not with indented *wave*, prone on the
' ground as now:' and v. 502, ' Spires that on the grass *floated*.'

If what happens to animals of the serpent kind, may hap- § 192.
pen to the human nerves, i. e. that they may be put into har- *Soul har-*
monic undulations by the agency of external objects, then was the *monic.*
opinion of Plato, that the soul was made according to harmony,
not without foundation; which opinion he might perhaps be led
into, by seeing the extraordinary effects daily produced by music,
partly owing to a more favourable climate, and partly owing to a
superior skill in the artists of those days. To the same purpose,
Aristid. Quint. p. 107. says, ' If our minds are affected by the
' vibrations of musical strings, where is the wonder? since the
' mind has a body belonging to it, resembling a musical instru-
' ment; and since we know that if a light body be placed on a
' string while an unison to it is sounded, the light body will move.'
And thus Lord Bacon, either induced by Platonic notions, or by
what he saw and felt himself, even in this unfavourable climate,
says, Advancem. of Learn. b. 2. ' This variable composition of
' man's body hath made it as an instrument easy to distemper;
                ' therefore

APPENDIX. 'therefore the poets did well to conjoin music and medicine in
'Apollo, because the office of medicine is but to tune this curi-
'ous harp of man's body, and to reduce it to harmony.' But
something else is required besides a musical instrument and a musician, in order to produce the proper effects of music. Nobody,
I think, will scruple to call Æolus's harp a musical instrument;
yet every gale will not shew the power of it; nor can every voice
nor every hand, though musical, raise those undulations in the
nerves, which are capable of inspiring rapture and enthusiasm.
Perhaps, if every circumstance besides was just what it ought to be,
want of simplicity alone might render the effect imperfect. This
appears to be Tartini's way of thinking; and even Dr. Wallis
lays so much stress upon simplicity, that he almost seems to have
been inclined to believe the relations of the effects of antient music, at least amongst the rustics, on this account chiefly.

§ 193. So much for the human soul as far as harmony is concerned.
Beasts affected But are the effects of music confined to man only? By no
by music. means: I will produce a few instances of the power of music over
the brute creation; and such instances as cannot be disputed. It
has been mentioned by several writers, Clemens Alexandrinus,
Ælian, Martianus Capella, that deer are affected by music; and
Waller, in a poem addressed to lady Isabella playing on the lute,
alludes to this notion in the following lines:

    There Love takes stand, and as she charms the ear,

    Empties his quiver on the list'ning deer.

I believe this allusion has generally been looked upon as a poetical
ornament, built upon a fabulous piece of natural history; I myself looked upon it in that light till I met with the following
passage in Playford's introduction to music, who seems to have
been a plain man, and one whose testimony might be taken. Thus
he says: 'Myself, as I travelled some years since near Royston,
    'met

'met a herd of stags, about 20, upon the road, following a bag-
'pipe and violin; which while the music played, they went
'forward; when it ceased they all stood still; and in this manner
'they were brought out of Yorkshire to Hampton-Court.'—
That sheep are affected by music, is no less certain. Apollonius
Rhodius, lib. 1. v. 574. says, ' As when a flock of sheep returning
'at evening to the fold, croud about the heels of the shepherd,
'who walks before, and plays a delightful pastoral air upon his
'sprightly pipe.'—And scripture evidently alludes to this custom
in more places than one, as Numbers xxvii. 17. May *lead* the people, that the congregation of the Lord be not as sheep which have
no shepherd. Again, Psal. lxxx. 1. Thou that *leadest* Joseph like
a flock. If I am not much mistaken, this custom still prevails in
some parts of the East, and certainly gave rise to the shepherd's
pipe, so frequently mentioned in the scenes of pastoral life.—Bees,
I think, may be put amongst the animals that delight in music.
Aristotle, vol. 1. p. 948. says, what is very well known, that they
are drawn together into the hive by the tinkling of brass, but
doubts whether from fear or pleasure. However others, as Pliny,
are of opinion that it is from pleasure. Lib. 11. § 22. And Varro calls
bees, the birds of the muses; de re rusticâ, lib. 3. § 16. What to
say of horses, I am not altogether without doubt. They are represented by some writers as delighting merely in the noise and clash of
arms; so Pindar calls the Sicilian horses τιδ ηροχαρμαι, Pyth. 2. 4.
and Virgil Georg. 3. 82. Tûm si qua sonum procul arma dedere,
&c. But I am apt to think the account given in the book of Job
is more natural, where the horse is described as saying among the
trumpets, Ha! ha! or, as the Septuagint gives it, Euge! which
translated according to our present way of expression, means,
Bravo! This is fine! It is added indeed, that he smells the battle, as appears by his prancing and neighing, according to the ver-
sion of the Septuagint, which seems better than that of our bible;
but

APPENDIX. but surely his prancing and neighing is accounted for sufficiently by the sound of the trumpets. Thus Ovid, 'Fremit equus quum 'signa dedit tubicen.'

§ 194.
Serpents affected by music.
I come now to some instances of the power of music on the brute creation, much more extraordinary than any hitherto by me mentioned, and full as well attested. It is a common practice in the East Indies, as I am assured, when a hooded serpent gets into a house, to send for a charmer, who with his pipe tempts him out of his hole, and after some time lulls him to sleep, and so seizes him. Scripture plainly alludes to something of this kind, in Psal. lviii. 4, 5. Like the deaf adder that stoppeth his ears: which refuseth to hear the voice of the charmer (αϕονος), charm he never so wisely. But we have an account in an author of credit still more wonderful. Nieuhoff, (in Churchhill's Voyages, vol. 2. p. 231.) speaking of Malabar, says, 'You meet there with certain 'vagabonds, who carry serpents in a basket, with some bran for 'their food, hanging on a stick, carried on the shoulders of two 'fellows; some of these serpents are six or nine feet long, of a grass 'green colour, and not above an inch thick; some are very large 'and bulky, with grey spots; so soon as these Malabar vagabonds 'begin to play upon a certain instrument, like a bagpipe, the 'serpents set themselves upright upon their tails, twist themselves 'in a most surprising manner, and soon after raise their fins or 'bristles which are near the head, and fall on with such fury, as 'if they would tear one another in pieces, to the no small terror 'of the spectators.' I desire to know, if any one, after reading this account, can think it reasonable to disbelieve the most extraordinary accounts of the power of music over the human mind, related by the antients, who were eye-witnesses of what they relate. Those who are versed in natural history would be able, in all probability, to increase the list of animals that delight in music: For my part I have none to add but the grasshopper, (different no doubt

[145]

doubt from what we call so) of which there is a pretty fable in Plato, vid. Phæd. towards the beginning: and the class of birds, many of which are so remarkable for singing, that Lucretius imagined they first taught mankind the art of music; Et liquidas avium voces imitarier ante, &c. lib. 5. v. 1378.

APPENDIX.

But this is not the full extent of harmony according to the Pythagoreans and Platonicians. They supposed the universe itself and all its parts to be formed by the principles of harmony. Nor do I imagine they meant only to make use of a figurative expression. There are traces of the harmonic principle scattered up and down, sufficient to make us look on it as one of the great and reigning principles of the inanimate world; and though we have no proof, or indeed any reason to believe that the Greeks were acquainted with the foundation of some of their philosophical opinions; yet what that very sagacious and judicious philosopher Mr. Maclaurin observes, Phil. Discov. of Newton, &c. p. 35. concerning the astronomy of Pythagoras, seems highly probable. 'When we find,' says he, ' their accounts (i. e. of the Greeks) ' to be very imperfect, it seems reasonable to suppose that they ' had some hints—only from some more knowing nations, who ' had made greater advances in philosophy, &c.' Those more knowing nations I suppose to have been the Ægyptians, from whom the first and great outlines of every art and science originally came. Maclaurin gives us one instance of the Pythagorean doctrine which could hardly be supposed to be of Greek original, the harmony of the spheres, and which, in conformity with Dr. Gregory, he explains as follows: ' If we should suppose musical chords ' extended from the sun to each planet; that all these chords ' might become unison, it would be requisite to increase or dimi- ' nish their tensions in the same proportions as would be sufficient ' to render the gravities of the planets equal; and from the simi- ' litude

§ 195. *Inanimate world harmonic.*

U

APPENDIX. 'litude of thofe proportions, the celebrated doctrine of the har-
'mony of the fpheres is fuppofed to have been derived.' Certain as this harmonic coincidence is now become, till Sir Ifaac Newton demonftrated the laws of gravitation in relation to the planets, it muft have paffed for the dream of an Utopian philofopher.

§ 196.
Colours harmonic.
Befides the above-mentioned inftance, which proves the harmony of the univerfe to be true in a literal fenfe; and which we fuppofe to have been known to the antients; there is another inftance totally new, difcovered alfo by Newton, equally ftriking, and equally extenfive. He found that the breadths of the feven original colours, were in the fame proportion as the feven mufical intervals that compofe an octave. The reafon why this law was followed rather than any other, does not appear; nor has Newton given any the leaft conjecture about it: but we cannot avoid believing that it tends fome way or other to the perfection of the univerfe, either as to ufe or beauty; and that the proportions cannot be altered, without altering the phænomena for the worfe, unlefs we can believe that the proportions of the elements alfo might be altered without any bad effect.

§ 197.
All fubftances elaftic, &c. are harmonic.
The inftances I have hitherto given of the harmonic principle prevailing in the inanimate fubftances of the univerfe, have been much more taken notice of, both as making part of the fublimeft philofophy that ever was invented, and alfo as being found in the greateft and moft interefting objects in nature; but the fame principle appears, if not with equal luftre, yet not with lefs certainty on many other occafions, and in a manner more intimately connected with mufic, both as to theory and practice; for all fubftances elaftic, homogeneous, and continuous, whether animal, vegetable or mineral, yield, upon percuffion, harmonic founds, i. e. they ring according to the common phrafe. This is notoriously

the

the cafe of iron, brafs, earthen-ware, glafs, wood, parchment, &c. and this happens, whatever their form may be. Nor is this owing to the motion produced in the air; for the fame thing will happen, without any communication between the organs of hearing and the air. Faften a ftring to a poker, or any iron bar, hold the ftring between your teeth in fuch a manner that the poker may fwing freely, ftop your ears clofe, make it ftrike againft the fender, and you will hear a loud clear ringing, as of a bell; nay, even the fire-pan, oddly fhaped as it may feem for fuch a purpofe, will produce much the fame effect: but the tongs, which are not a continuous body, make only a confufed and indiftinct noife. This experiment is fo very common, and well known, that I remember to have diverted myfelf frequently with it when a child. Lord Keeper North mentions an experiment, which proves likewife, that we may feel mufic without the medium of air. In his Philof. Effay on Mufic, p. 16. he fays thus: ' Such a continuity to the nerve of hearing will caufe a fenfe of ' found to a man that hath ftopped his ears, if he will hold a ' ftick that touches the founding inftrument between his teeth.'

APPENDIX.

Since then it appears that it has pleafed the Supreme Being to form many of his wondrous works according to the principles of harmony, and fince it is certain that fome of our pureft and moft affecting pleafures arife from harmony, can it be looked upon as unbecoming to give up fome of our time to the ftudy of an act manifeftly intended by Providence to allure us to the love of order, &c. according to the doctrine of Plato? Surely not: and the lefs fo, as mufic has, not without reafon, been thought to contribute to the cure of fome difeafes. Baglivi, p. 363, fays; Aliis morbis confert mufica, &c. Again, ib. Exercitatio vocis debito cantu ad plures conducit morbos, ut fufe monet Hippocrates, 3. diæ. n. 16. et multo melius de infomniis, n. 3. And

§ 198.
Mufic ought to be ftudied.

APPENDIX. the same Baglivi, p. 390, has a chapter intitled, De methodo curandi morbos complures musicâ, saltatione, &c. I say nothing about the tarantula, because the facts have been disputed; how justly I know not. It is certain, that Baglivi and his father, both of Calabria, (the scene of the supposed phænomenon) and both eminent physicians, did believe them, as appears by the dissertation on that subject written by the former. But however that may be, I have no doubt about some nervous cases said to have been relieved, and even cured, by music.

§ 199.
Music causes sleep.

Plato observes, p. 881, that when mothers want to make their children sleep, the remedy they use is not silence and rest, but, on the contrary, dancing and tossing them about in their arms, and enchanting them, as it were, by songs: and people, he adds, who are possessed with a bacchanalian fury, are brought to their senses by the same method. The effect of sounds is very extraordinary, and very various. The Pythagoreans, of all men, seem to have understood this matter the best; and to have made use of it, on many occasions, to very good purposes. The stories and remains of that noble sect, are full of accounts that appear to us fabulous, but may nevertheless be true. Lord Bacon observes, Nat. Hist. Art. 112, that the wind, purling of water, humming of bees, a sweet voice of one that reads, &c. are opiates. Now that these sounds, though not perhaps in themselves, strictly speaking, harmonic, may yet put the nerves into harmonic undulations, appears by the phænomenon of Æolus' harp. The only difference is, that the air strikes upon the strings of the harp already tuned; whereas, it strikes upon the nerves perhaps out of tune. But this difference is of no consequence; for the soul has a power of adjusting the auditory organs to any pitch requisite, as is evident whenever a musician changes the key abruptly; for in that case, it is some time before the ear can comprehend the harmony. Analogous phænomena,

nomena, in relation to the organs of singing and seeing, prove the truth of my assertion. It is therefore highly probable, that in some cases, what produces harmonic undulations in the nerves, will produce sleep; and that was the opinion of Pindar, who, in his sublime Pythic ode, (finely imitated by one of our poets) speaking of the eagle, says:

<blockquote>
Perch'd on the sceptre of the Olympian king,
The thrilling darts of harmony he feels;
And indolently hangs his rapid wing,
While gentle sleep his closing eyelids seals;
And o'er his heaving limbs, in loose array,
To ev'ry balmy gale the ruffling feathers play.
West's PINDAR.
</blockquote>

Appendix.

This effect of harmony, the reason of which is not difficult to assign, were it constant, would be of the greatest consequence; for to produce sleep, in some disorders, is to produce a cure.

§ 200. *Horrible sounds.*

I cannot omit, on this occasion, to mention the opposite effect of discordant sounds, as contraries illustrate one another best. Charlevoix, speaking of the Indians of Canada, lett. 13. says, ' That their war-songs are at all times melancholy and doleful; ' but here they were to the last degree frightful; occasioned per- ' haps, he adds, entirely by the darkness of the night, and the ap- ' proaches of the festival.' I believe Charlevoix is mistaken in his conjecture about the cause of the effect mentioned; for Anson's Voyage, p. 30. says, ' That Orellana placed his hands hollow to ' his mouth, and bellowed out the war-cry used by those savages, ' which is said to be the harshest and most terrifying sound known ' in nature. This hideous yell, &c.' And Plutarch, speaking of the Parthians, when they attacked Crassus, says, ' They do not ' use horns or trumpets in war; but by means of hollow clubs, ' covered with leather, and having bells fastened to them, the ' Parthians spread a din far and wide. These instruments send ' forth

APPENDIX. 'forth a deep and terrible sound, something between the howling
'of wild beasts and the harshness of thunder. This custom the
'Parthians use, as knowing, that of all the senses the hearing is
'the most capable of disordering the mind, and that its operations
'have the quickest effect. The Romans, upon hearing these
'horrible sounds, threw down their arms.' Plut. Vol. I. p. 557.
But to return from the gloomy scenes of horror and discord to
those of cheerfulness and harmony.

§ 201. It appears from a variety of conclusive circumstances, that music
Music accompanies content, &c. is the voice of industry—of content—of serenity—of innocence.—
In short, it is the voice of nature, uncorrupted and unoppressed;
and as such is heard, and once was more frequently heard, in our
fields and villages. When it is considered in this light, it is of
all harmonies the most delightful; as such, it has struck men of
the most delicate sensations.—The plowman whistling o'er the
furrowed land—the milkmaid singing blithe—the spinsters, and
the knitters in the sun—and the free maids, that weave their thread
with bone, chaunting, were objects that drew the attention of two
of the greatest poets the world has known. But agreeable as these
effusions of the heart may be to the ear of every man who has feeling;
yet since it has pleased our good and great Creator, to grant us
faculties capable of improving the imperfect sallies of nature, I
cannot conceive why we ought not to go a step farther, and learn
music as an art, and even make it a regular part of education,
as was antiently the custom of many wise nations. I would
not willingly incur the censure of some grave and sober people,
who think we have already but too much of such trifling and useless amusements: I must therefore explain myself.

§ 202. My opinion is, that young ladies at least, who have a tolerable
Young ladies should learn music. ear, to say nothing of the other sex, should learn music. But as
I do not recommend it to them for the purpose of parade and
ostentation,

oftentation, fo I should not wifh to have them attempt to rival the- APPENDIX.
atrical performers, either in finging or playing. A proper model
to imitate on this occafion, may be feen § 181. where the paffage
quoted from Plato recommends only the fimpleft kind of mufic
for the education of youth. In his books of laws, p. 893, he propofes, that they fhould begin at thirteen years of age, and continue
for three years, and no longer. Something of this fort might perhaps fuit our young ladies in general. It feems fufficient that
they learn mufic enough to form their ear, and to be able to pick
out an eafy tune, by the help of fome manageable and portable inftrument, as the guitar; and particularly that they learn to tune it
well. Their bufinefs fhould be to practife merely for the amufements
of themfelves, their own family, and particular friends, or rather
for domeftic comfort, which they were by Providence defigned to
promote; viz. To calm the boifterous paffions—to relieve the
anxieties and cares of life—to infpire cheerfulnefs—to appeafe the
nerves, when irritated by pain, ficknefs, or labour of mind or
body, to footh the peevifhnefs of infancy and old age—and to
raife the mind to a feeling and love of order. She who fhall im-
prove the natural talents, with which women are born, of doing
all thefe things, will not have mifpent her time by applying three
years to mufic. How it ferves thofe noble purpofes, as now practifed, I leave others to tell.

That the divine gift of mufic was in a great meafure intended § 203.
for the purpofes above-mentioned, feems clear from the courfe of *Mufical dif-*
nature in other animals. The birds, who, except man, are almoft *cord.*
the only fongfters in the creation, hardly ever fing but to relieve the
tedioufnefs of incubation in the female; infomuch, that whereever
you hear a bird fing, you may be generally fure that there is a neft
not far off. It is natural to inquire, on this occafion, why the fongs
of various birds finging together are not difagreeable, as being neceffarily

APPENDIX. cessarily discordant. To this I answer, that I do not believe they are discordant: Why should we not suppose, that the delicate ear of the birds produces the same effect as we daily find amongst men, who, however many in number, constantly fall into consonant tones in conversing with one another? I never knew but one instance to the contrary; and that instance proved the truth of my assertion: for there was something so unharmonious and harsh in his speech merely on that account, that every body was offended with his want of ear, and wondered at it. The same solution serves for Shakespeare's musical discord, as he calls it, speaking of the cry of a pack of hounds. Midsummer Night's Dream.

§ 204.
Religious Music.

I find it difficult to quit this enchanted ground, surrounded as I am by sirens on every side, who are tempting me to quit my course; but reason seems to beckon me away, and point to the port in view. However, I hear the voice of one who must be obeyed. Urania whispers me about music employed in the pure worship of God, 1 Chron. xxiii. 5. and 2 Chron. v. 12, 13.—of prophets prophesying, with a psaltery, and a tabret, and a pipe, and a harp before them, 1 Chron. xxv. 3.—of injunctions to sing praises to God, Psal. xxxiii. 2. cl. 3, &c. Ephes. v. 19. Coloss. iii. 16.—of saints harping and singing before the throne of God—of music accompanying the creation, Job xxxviii. 7.—the redemption, Luke ii. 13.—the resurrection, 1 Cor. xv. 52. After what I have cited from scripture, it may seem quite unnecessary to add a word farther on this subject; but such is the weight and authority of one whose opinion I am going to produce, and so ably is his opinion drawn up, that I think every reader will approve of my enriching this treatise with it; especially, as it not only relates to the last article, but to many other essential parts of the whole system of music. The writer I mean is Hooker; who, in his Eccles. Polit. lib. v. artic. 38. says as follows:

'Touching

'Touching musical harmony, whether by instrument or by voice, it being but of high and low in sounds, a due proportionable disposition, such notwithstanding is the force thereof, and so pleasing effects it hath in that very part of man which is most divine, that some have been thereby induced to think that the soul itself by nature is, or hath in it harmonie; a thing which delighteth all ages, and beseemeth all states; a thing as seasonable in grief as in joy; as decent being added unto actions of greatest weight and solemnitie, as being used when men most sequester themselves from action. The reason hereof is an admirable facilitie which music hath to expresse and represente to the minde, more inwardly than any other sensible meane, the very standing, rising and falling, the very steps and inflections every way, the turnes and varieties of all passions whereunto the minde is subject; yea so to imitate them, that whether it resemble unto us the same state wherein our mindes alreadie are, or a cleane contrarie, we are not more contentedly by the one confirmed, then changed and led away by the other.

APPENDIX.

§. 205.
Hooker on musíc.

'In harmonie, the very image and character of vertue and vice is perceived, the minde delighted with their resemblances, and brought, by having them often iterated, into a love of the things themselves. For which cause, there is nothing more contagious and pestilent than some kindes of harmonie; than some, nothing more strong and potent unto good. And that there is such a difference of one kinde from another, we need no proof but our own experience; in as much as we are at the hearing of some more inclined unto sorrow and heavinels; of some more mollified and softened in minde; one apter to stay and settle us; another, to move and stir our affections: there is that draweth to a marvellous, grave, and sober mediocritie; there is also that carryeth, as it were, into ecstasies, filling the

§ 206.

'minde

APPENDIX. ' minde with a heavenly joy, and for the time in a manner
' fevering it from the body, So that, although we lay altogether
' afide the confideration of dittie or matter, the very harmonie of
' founds being framed in due fort, and carryed from the ear to the
' fpiritual faculties of our foules, is, by a native puiffance and ef-
' ficacie, greatly availeable to bring to a perfect temper, whatfo-
' ever is there troubled ; apt as well to quicken the fpirits, as to
' allay that which is too eager ; foveraignne againft mellancholy
' and defpair ; forcible to draw forth teares of devotion, if the
' minde be fuch as can yeeld them ; able both to move and to
' moderate all affections. The prophet David having therefore
' fingular knowledge, not in poetrie alone, but in mufique alfo,
' judged them both to be things moft neceffarie for the houfe of
' God, left behinde him, to that purpofe, a number of divinelie in-
' dited poemes ; and was farther the author of adding unto poe-
' trie melodie in publique prayer, melodie both vocal and inftru-
' mental, for the raifing up of mens harts, and the fweetning of
' their affections towards God.'

F I N I S.

I N D E X

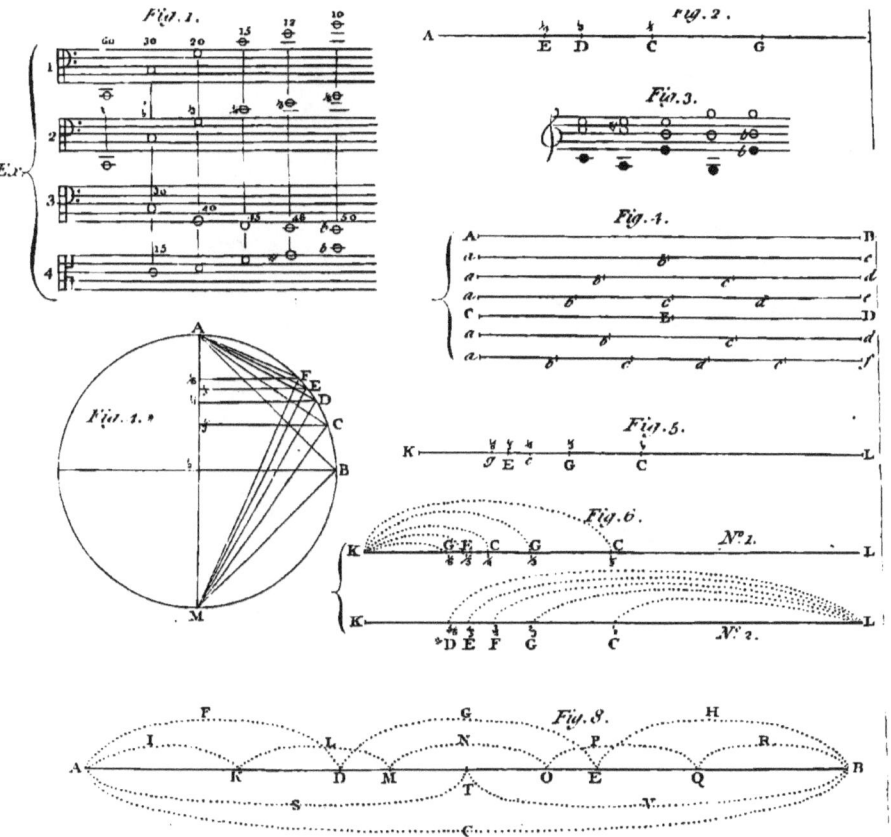

INDEX.

N. B. The Numbers refer to the Sections.

A.

ACCENTS, musical and metrical, 79.
Ægyptian music, 168, 169; sculpture and painting, 173, 174.
Air, undulations in it, 17.
Amphion, 182.
Animal spirits, 189.
Aristoxenus, music in his time, 180.
Arithmetical notes, 39; found along with the harmonic, 41.
Author, how much indebted to Tartini, 47.

B.

Bacon, Lord, on the human body, 192.
Ballads, old, 122.
Bases, first, second, and third, 71.
Beasts affected by music, 193.
Bees affected by music, 193.
Birds, why and when they sing, 203; take the tone from one another, ibid.
Breaking of notes, 140.

INDEX.

C.
Cadences, 76.
Causes difficult to find, 68.
Charles, the famous performer on the horn, 155.
Chromatic, antient, 83.
Church music, old, 109. 111; corrupted, 110.
Cithara, 64.
Colors in harmonic proportion, 196.
Comma, musical, 56.
Counterpoint, 69.

D.
Dancing, 193.
David's harp, 63.
Deer, 193.
Diatonic, its perfection, 87.
Difficulty of finding causes, 68.
Discordant notes, 82; sounds, effect of them, 200.
Discords and dissonances, 45. 48, 49. 74. 162.
Discovery of musical intervals, 14.
Drum, 33.

E.
Effect of a scene of recitative, 91; of simultaneous harmony, 104—106.
Elastic bodies harmonic, 197.
Enharmonic, antient, 84; of Rameau, 85.
Errors leading to truth, 30.
Error, mathematical, 28.

F.
Figuring the octave, 70.
French horn, 2.

G.
Galileo confirms the musical ratios, by the pendulum, 16.
Grasshopper musical, 194.
Greatest common measure in a vibrating string, 40.
Greek music, 112. 175, 176. 179; its power, 91.

H.

INDEX.

H.
Hammers of Pythagoras, 12, 13.
Harmonic unity, 6; notes, 66.
Harmonic and arithmetical notes connected, 39; found together, 41.
Harmony deducible from Tartini's principles, 166; of the spheres, 195.
Harp, 59. 61—63; tuning it in a third major, 60; in a third minor, 151, 152.
Harp Æolus's, 65. 153—155. 199.
Harpsichord, 59.
Heptachord invented by Hermes, 170.
Homer, music in his time, 177; after, 178.
Hooker on music, 204.
Horse affected by music, 193.
Hounds take the tone from one another, 203.
Huygens's famous passage, 57, 58.

I.
Idæi Dactyli, 78.
Intervals musical, 11. 131, 132. 139; discovery of them, 14; by the pendulum, 16.; their cause, 19; ascending and descending, 134—137.

K.
Kepler fond of analogies, 27.

L.
Lacedæmonian music, 185; senatus-consultum, 106.
Lyre, 63.

M.
Measure or time, 75. 102.
Mersennus discovered three sounds in a string, 24.
Metre, 77.
Mixed scale, 73.
Modes, antient, 72; of the Greeks, 89, 112; modern, 93.; old Italian, 89. 94; their number, 95; antient and modern compared, 96.

Modulation,

INDEX.

Modulation, modern, 115—118. 156. 163, 164.
Monochord compared with the trumpet-marine, 37.
Music, its power proved by theory, 187; beasts affected by it, 193; deer—sheep—bees—horses, ibid; horses, 194; causes sleep, 199; rustic agreeable, 201; ladies ought to learn it, 202; religious, 204; deserves to be studied, 198; cures diseases, ibid; perfect, 65; Persian, 77; principles wanting amongst moderns, 92; old church, 109. 111; corrupted, 110; Greek, 175, 176. 179; unknown, 113; simple, best, 122; Ægyptian, 168, 169; in the time of Homer, 177; after him, 178; in the time of Aristoxenus, 180; in parts, 181; antient, its power, 184.

N.

Nervous system, 188.
Newton's colours, 196.
North, Lord Keeper, an observation of his, 154; another, 197.
Notes of the octave how found, 46; breaking of, 140.
Noting of music, 10.
Numbers expressing the disjunct tetrachord known to the Chaldeans, 13.

O.

Octachord invented by Hermes, 171; its advantages, 172.
Octave, 15. 51—53. 139.
Old ballads, 122.
Old Italian modes, 94.
Olympus's music, 183.
Organ, 4.
Orpheus, stories about him, 182.
Oscillation of strings, 5.

P.

Painting, Ægyptian, 173, 174.
Passions, how to be imitated, 101; how moved, 126—130.
Pendulum, 16.
Perfect music, 65.
Persian music, 77.

Playford,

INDEX.

Playford, a story about deer, 193.
Points of rest in a vibrating string, 21—23.
Poker, a phænomenon of it, 197.
Power of music from theory, 187; of Greek, 91—184.
Practical treatise on music wanting, 165.
Principles of music wanting amongst the moderns, 92.
Problem, mathematical, 32; physico-mathematical, 43.
Prosody, 97—100; Italian, 81; English, ibid.
Ptolemy's prejudice about the circle, 27; true intervals of the octave found by him, 15.
Pythagoras's story about his settling the disjunct tetrachord, 12, 13.

R.

Rameau's enharmonic, 84.
Resolution of discords, 48, 49.
Rules deduced from Tartini's principles, 167.
Rythm, 78, 80.

S.

Seasons of the year harmonic, 13.
Senatus-consultum, Lacedæmonian, 186.
Serpents, regular undulations of, 191; affected by music, 194.
Sheep affected by music, 193.
Simultaneous harmony, 103, 108; effect of it, 104, 105, 106; not used by the Greeks, 107.
Soul, material, 187; harmonic, 192.
Spheres, harmony of them, 195.
Strings, oscillation of them, 5; in motion, give 3d and 5th, 16; observed first by Marsennus, 24.

T.

Taste, 123—125.
Tasto-fermo, 120, 121.
Temperament, 55, 56; of Valloti, 55.
Third major, 143, 144; minor, 142, 145—149, 157—161; difference between them, 133, 137.
Third sounds, 7, 8; in the third minor, 44, 45.

Tone,

INDEX.

Tone, a good, on the violin, 66.
Tritones, 86.
Trumpet-marine, 2, 3. 25. 35, 36. 67.

U.

Undulations in air, 17; in water, ibid; in serpents, 191.

V.

Vibrations, 190; in wood, 18.

W.

Waller's observation on deer, 193.
Wallis, points of rest in a vibrating string, 21—23.]

www.ingramcontent.com/pod-product-compliance
Lightning Source LLC
Chambersburg PA
CBHW020307170426
43202CB00008B/522